Guide to ship sanitation

Third edition

Geneva 2011

WHO Library Cataloguing-in-Publication Data:

World Health Organization.

WHO *Guide to ship sanitation*. 3rd ed.

1. Ships 2. Public health 3. Sanitation 4. Disease transmission—prevention and control 5. Communicable disease control—methods 6. Guidelines I. Title.

ISBN 978 92 4 154669 0 (NLM classification: WA 810)

Printed in France

Cover design by Crayonbleu, Lyon, France
Layout by Biotext Pty Ltd, Canberra, Australia

Contents

Tables

Figures

Foreword

Historically, ships have played a significant role in the global transmission of infectious disease. Some of the earliest recorded evidence of attempts to control human disease transmission via ships dates to the 14th century, when ports denied access to ships suspected of carrying the plague. In the 19th century, the spread of cholera pandemics was thought to have been facilitated by merchant shipping. A World Health Organization (WHO) review identified more than 100 disease outbreaks associated with ships between 1970 and 2003 (Rooney et al., 2004).

Today's world fleet of propelled seagoing merchant ships of more than 100 billion tonnes comprises 99 741 ships, with an average age of 22 years, registered in more than 150 nations and crewed by more than a million seafarers of virtually every nationality (IHS Fairplay, 2010). World seaborne trade figures suggest that the amount of goods loaded on ships has increased considerably in recent decades; in 2007, it reached 7.3 billion tonnes, a volume increase of 4.8% over the previous year (United Nations, 2008). During the three decades to 2008, the annual average growth rate of world seaborne trade was estimated at 3.1% (United Nations, 2008). The shipping industry also supports tourism and recreation. American cruise ships alone carried 13.4 million people during 2009, for an average period of 7.3 days per person, a passenger number increase averaging 4.7% per year over the preceding four years (Cruise Lines International Association, 2010). Naval ships also carry considerable numbers of crew, sometimes more than 5000 per ship. Ferries are ubiquitous around the world in port cities and at some river crossings and are used by many people on a daily basis.

Because of the international nature of ship transport, international regulations relating to sanitary aspects of ship transport have been in place for more than half a century. The International Sanitary Regulations of 1951 were replaced by the International Health Regulations (IHR) adopted by WHO in 1969. The IHR were revised at the Fifty-eighth World Health Assembly in 2005.

The WHO *Guide to ship sanitation* has become the official WHO global reference on health requirements for ship construction and operation. Its original purpose was to standardize the sanitary measures taken in ships, to safeguard the health of travellers and workers and to prevent the spread of infection from one country to another. Today, however, given the number of specific guidance documents, conventions and regulations currently available that provide full accounts of the design and operational detail relating to ships, the primary aim of the guide is to present the public health significance of ships in terms of disease and to highlight the importance of applying appropriate control measures.

The guide was first published in 1967 and amended in 1987. This revised third edition of the guide has been prepared to reflect the changes in construction, design and size of ships since the 1960s and the existence of new diseases (e.g. legionellosis) that were not foreseen when the 1967 guide was published.

The guide has been developed through an iterative series of drafting and peer-review steps. In revising the guide, expert meetings were held in Miami, United States of America (USA), on 3–4 October 2001 and in Vancouver, Canada, on 8–10 October 2002 to discuss and recommend the proposed contents. Expert meetings to review the draft guide were held on 25 October 2007 in Montreal, Canada, and on 12–13 October 2009 in Lyon, France. Participants represented cruise ship operators, seafarer associations, collaborating member states for the IHR 2005, port state control, port health authorities and other regulatory agencies. A complete list of contributors to the guide can be found in the Acknowledgements section.

The *Guide to ship sanitation* and the *International medical guide for ships* (WHO, 2007) are companion volumes oriented towards preventive health and curative health, respectively, on board ships.

Acknowledgements

The preparation of this third edition of the *Guide to ship sanitation* involved the participation of many experts from diverse developing and developed countries.

The work was facilitated greatly by the existence of prior editions and by a systematic review of outbreaks on board ships prepared by Dr Roisin Rooney, WHO, Geneva, which was previously published by WHO (2001).

The international branch of the National Sanitation Foundation, Ann Arbor, USA, seconded a staff member to WHO Geneva whose main line of activity was the initial development of this guide.

The work of the following individuals was crucial to the development of this edition of the *Guide to ship sanitation* and is gratefully acknowledged:

J. Adams, Fisheries and Oceans Canada, Ottawa, Canada

J. Ames, Centers for Disease Control and Prevention, Atlanta, USA

D. Antunes, North Regional Health Authority, Lisbon, Portugal

J. Bainbridge, International Transport Workers' Federation, London, England

J. Barrow, Centers for Disease Control and Prevention, Atlanta, USA

J. Bartram, WHO, Geneva, Switzerland

D. Bennitz, Health Canada, Ottawa, Canada

R. Bos, WHO, Geneva, Switzerland

G. Branston, Port Health Services, East London, South Africa

B. Brockway, Southampton City Council, Southampton, England

C. Browne, Ministry of Health, St Michael, Barbados, West Indies

R. Bryant, Chamber of Shipping of British Columbia, Vancouver, Canada

L.A. Campos, National Sanitary Control Agency (ANVISA), Brasília, Brazil

Y. Chartier, WHO, Geneva, Switzerland

L. Chauham, Ministry of Health, New Delhi, India

S. Cocksedge, WHO, Geneva, Switzerland

J. Colligan, Maritime and Coastguard Agency, Edinburgh, Scotland

J. Cotruvo, Joseph Cotruvo & Associates LLC, Washington, USA

P.B. Coury, National Sanitary Control Agency (ANVISA), Brasília, Brazil

E. Cramer, Centers for Disease Control and Prevention, Atlanta, USA

M.H. Figueiredo da Cunha, National Sanitary Control Agency (ANVISA), Brasília, Brazil

F.M. da Rocha, National Sanitary Control Agency (ANVISA), Brasília, Brazil

D. Davidson, Food and Drug Administration, College Park, USA

D. Dearsley, International Shipping Federation, London, England

T. Degerman, Kvaerner Masa-Yards, Turku, Finland

S. Deno, International Council of Cruise Lines, Arlington, USA

M. do Céu Madeira, Directorate General of Health, Lisbon, Portugal

X. Donglu, Ministry of Health, Beijing, China

B. Elliott, Transport Canada, Ottawa, Canada

Z. Fang, Department of Health Quarantine, General Administration of Quality Supervision, Inspection and Quarantine (AQSIQ), Beijing, China

M. Ferson, South Eastern Sydney Public Health Unit, Randwick, Australia

D. Forney, Centers for Disease Control and Prevention, Atlanta, USA

M.V. Gabor, Ministry of Public Health, Montevideo, Uruguay

B. Gau, Hamburg Port Health Center, Hamburg, Germany

R. Griffin, Food Standards Agency, London, England

C. Hadjichristodoulou, University of Thessaly, Larissa, Greece

J. Hansen, North West Cruiseship Association, Vancouver, Canada

J. Harb, Health Canada, Vancouver, Canada

D. Hardy, Navy Environmental Health Center, Norfolk, USA

D. Harper, Centers for Disease Control and Prevention, Atlanta, USA

L. Hope, WHO, Geneva, Switzerland (seconded by NSF International, Ann Arbor, USA)

H. Kong, Department of Health, Hong Kong Special Administrative Region, China

D. Kurnaev, Health Ministry, Centre of State Sanitary Epidemiological Survey on Water and Air Transport for the North-Western Region of Russia, St Petersburg, Russian Federation

I. Lantz, Shipping Federation of Canada, Montreal, Canada

M. Libel, Pan American Health Organization, WHO Regional Office, Washington, USA

J. Maniram, Port Health Manager, Kwazulu, South Africa

D.L. Menucci, WHO, Lyon, France

J. Michalowski, United States Coast Guard, Washington, USA

S. Minchang, State Administration for Entry–Exit Inspection and Quarantine of People's Republic of China, Beijing, China

H.G.H. Mohammad, Ministry of Health, Rumaithiya, Kuwait

K. Montonen, Kvaerner Masa-Yards, Turku, Finland

B. Mouchtouri, University of Thessaly, Larissa, Greece

E. Mourab, Ministry of Health and Population, Cairo, Egypt

M. Moussif, Mohamed V Airport, Casablanca, Morocco

J. Nadeau, Health Canada, Ottawa, Canada

R. Neipp, Ministry of Health and Social Policy, Madrid, Spain

M. O'Mahony, Department of Health, London, England

B. Patterson, Health Canada, Vancouver, Canada

T. Paux, Ministry of Health, Paris, France

M. Plemp, Centre for Infectious Disease Control, National Institute for Public Health and the Environment, Amsterdam, the Netherlands

K. Porter, Environmental Protection Agency, Washington, USA

T. Pule, Ministry of Health, Pretoria, South Africa

R. Rooney, WHO, Geneva, Switzerland

P. Rotheram, Association of Port Health Authorities, Runcorn, England

S. Ruitai, Ministry of Health, Beijing, China

G. Sam, Department of Health and Aged Care, Canberra, Australia

J. Sarubbi, United States Coast Guard, Washington, USA

T. Sasso, International Transport Workers' Federation, Cape Canaveral, Florida, USA

R. Schiferli, Secretariat of the Paris Memorandum of Understanding on Port State Control, The Hague, the Netherlands

C. Schlaich, Hamburg Port Health Center, Hamburg, Germany

C. Sevenich, Port Health Authority, Hamburg, Germany

E. Sheward, University of Central Lancashire, West Sussex, England

R. Suraj, Navy Environmental Health Center, Norfolk, USA

H. Thakore, Health Canada, Vancouver, Canada

T. Thompson, International Council of Cruise Lines, Arlington, USA

D.M. Trindade, Centre for Disease Control and Prevention, Macao Special Administrative Region, China

V. Vuttivirojana, Ministry of Public Health, Nonthaburi, Thailand

B. Wagner, International Labour Organization, Geneva, Switzerland

M. Wahab, Ministry of Health and Population, Cairo, Egypt

R. Wahabi, Ministry of Health, Rabat-Mechquar, Morocco

N. Wang, WHO, Lyon, France

S. Westacott, Port Health Services, Southampton City Council, Southampton, England

T. Whitehouse, Canadian Coast Guard, Ottawa, Canada

A. Winbow, International Maritime Organization, London, England

N. Wiseman, International Shipping Federation, London, England

P. Ward, A. Rivière, N. Wang and D.L. Menucci provided secretarial and administrative support throughout the meetings during the development of the guide. D. Deere (Water Futures, University of New South Wales, Sydney, Australia, and Water Quality Research Australia) and M. Sheffer (Ottawa, Canada) undertook technical writing and editing roles in developing the guide. The preparation of this third edition of the guide would not have been possible without the generous support of the United States Department of Health and Human Services, the Swedish International Development Cooperation Agency and Health Canada.

Acronyms and abbreviations

AFR	accidental faecal release
AGI	acute gastrointestinal illness
ARI	acute respiratory illness
CCP	critical control point
cfu	colony-forming unit
FAO	Food and Agriculture Organization of the United Nations
FSP	food safety plan or food safety programme
GDWQ	*Guidelines for drinking-water quality*
HACCP	hazard analysis and critical control point
HPC	heterotrophic plate count
HVAC	heating, ventilation and air-conditioning
IEC	International Electrotechnical Commission
IHR	International Health Regulations
ILO	International Labour Organization
IMO	International Maritime Organization
ISO	International Organization for Standardization
MARPOL 73/78	International Convention for the Prevention of Pollution from Ships
SARS	severe acute respiratory syndrome
spp.	species
USA	United States of America
UV	ultraviolet
WHO	World Health Organization
WSP	water safety plan

1 Introduction

1.1 Significance of ships to health

Ships can have significance to public health beyond their role in ship-acquired infection. For example, ships can transport infected humans and other vectors, such as mosquitoes and rats, between ports and can therefore act as a means of national and international dissemination of disease and disease agents.

Historically, ships have played an important role in transmitting infectious diseases around the world. The spread of cholera pandemics in the 19th century was thought to be linked to trade routes and facilitated by merchant shipping. Efforts to control the movement of human disease on ships can be traced back to the Middle Ages, when, in 1377, Venice and Rhodes denied access to ships carrying passengers infected with the plague, giving rise to the term "quarantine". On arrival, travellers were detained in isolation for 40 days before they were allowed to proceed to their final destination. Overcrowding on ships, filth and lack of personal hygiene were often associated with epidemics of rickettsial typhus fever. Preventive measures, such as quarantine, delousing and maintaining personal cleanliness by use of soap, were gradually adopted, and the incidence of typhus decreased.

More than 100 outbreaks of infectious diseases associated with ships were reported between 1970 and 2003 (Rooney et al., 2004). Reported outbreaks included legionellosis, influenza, typhoid fever, salmonellosis, viral gastroenteritis (e.g. norovirus), enterotoxigenic *Escherichia coli* infection, shigellosis, cryptosporidiosis and trichinosis. Naval ships, cargo ships, ferries and cruise ships were all affected, often with serious operational and financial consequences.

These reported outbreaks represent just a small proportion of the total disease burden attributable to ship-acquired disease. For every notified and reported case listed in outbreak reports, there are likely to be many more cases that go unreported.

If proper control measures are not in place, ships are particularly prone to disease outbreaks. Ships contain isolated communities with close accommodations, shared sanitary facilities and common food and water supplies. Such conditions can be favourable to the spread of infectious diseases. The inevitable publicity that comes along with a disease outbreak on board can have a serious financial impact on the ship owners and those relying on use of the ship for transport or leisure.

It is estimated that 1.2 million seafarers are employed on ships around the world (IMO, 2009). As many spend months at sea, sometimes in remote regions of the world, cargo ships on long voyages contain particularly isolated communities. Good sanitary conditions on ships are crucial to both the health and the welfare of seafarers.

By taking sensible preventive control measures, it is possible to protect passengers, crew and the public at large from disease transmission related to ships. To the extent possible, control strategies should be targeted to minimizing contamination at source. From a public health perspective, the focus should be on proactive and preventive measures rather than reactive and curative. For example:

- the design and construction of the ship should be as failsafe as possible with respect to maintaining a sanitary environment;
- the food, water and materials taken on board should be as safe as possible;
- crew should be well trained in ship sanitation and have all the equipment, facilities, materials and capacity necessary to permit the maintenance of a sanitary environment on board;
- a risk management system should be put in place and maintained to ensure the identification, reporting and mitigation of public health risks.

1.2 Scope, purpose and objective

The primary aim of the revised *Guide to ship sanitation* is to present the public health significance of ships in terms of disease and to highlight the importance of applying appropriate control measures. The guide is intended to be used as a basis for the development of national approaches to controlling the hazards that may be encountered on ships, as well as providing a framework for policy-making and local decision-making. The guide may also be used as reference material for regulators, ship operators and ship builders, as well as a checklist for understanding and assessing the potential health impacts of projects involving the design of ships.

In 1967, the World Health Organization (WHO) first published the *Guide to ship sanitation*, which was subjected to minor amendments in 1987. In the past, the guide was directly referenced in the International Health Regulations (IHR) (Article 14), and its purpose was to standardize the sanitary measures taken in relation to ships to safeguard the health of travellers and to prevent the spread of infection from one country to another.

The 1967 guide was based on the results of a survey of 103 countries and represented a synthesis of best national practices at the time. It covered potable water supply, swimming-pool safety, waste disposal, food safety and vermin control. Before publication, it was circulated to the International Labour Organization (ILO) and a number of other international agencies for comment. The guide supplemented the requirements of the IHR and was the official global reference for health requirements for ship construction and operation.

Since 1967, a number of specific guidance documents, conventions and regulations have evolved that provide full accounts of the design and operational detail relating to ships, and many take sanitation into consideration. To some extent, these have made the original purpose of the guide obsolete, and the purpose of this revised guide is different. The guide has not been explicitly referenced since the 2005 version of the IHR, hereafter referred to as IHR 2005 (WHO, 2005) (see section 1.3.1).

This document is intended to provide examples of accepted good practices. However, it is acknowledged that there may be equally effective alternative solutions that could be deployed to achieve the desired objectives. If alternative solutions are adopted, there is a need to provide objective evidence of their effectiveness. The primary consideration is that the results are effective.

1.3 Harmonization with other international regulations

1.3.1 International Health Regulations

The International Sanitary Regulations were developed in 1951 to prevent the spread of six infectious diseases: cholera, plague, yellow fever, smallpox, typhus and relapsing fever. These regulations were revised and renamed the International Health Regulations (IHR) in 1969.

The purpose of the IHR 2005 is "to prevent, protect against, control and provide a public health response to the international spread of disease in ways that are commensurate with and restricted to public health risks, and which avoid unnecessary interference with international traffic and trade".

The IHR were amended in 1973 and 1981. The diseases subject to these regulations were reduced to three: plague, yellow fever and cholera. In 1995, the World Health Assembly called for the regulations to be revised. The IHR were revised and presented to the Fifty-eighth World Health Assembly on 23 May 2005 (WHO, 2005).

The IHR 2005 apply to world traffic: ships, aircraft, other conveyances, travellers and cargoes. Ships and aircraft are discussed specifically in the *Guide to ship sanitation* and the *Guide to hygiene and sanitation in aviation* (WHO, 2009), respectively. The guides provide a summary of the health basis behind the IHR 2005 and help to bridge the gap between the regulations, as a legal document, and the practical aspects of implementation of appropriate practices.

Articles 22(b) and 24(c) of the IHR 2005 require State Parties to take all practicable measures to ensure that international conveyance operators keep their conveyances free from sources of contamination and infection, and competent authorities are responsible for ensuring that facilities at international ports (e.g. potable water, eating establishments, public washrooms, appropriate solid and liquid waste disposal services) are kept in sanitary condition.

Article 22(e) of the IHR 2005 states that the competent authority in each State Party is responsible for the supervised removal and safe disposal of any contaminated water or food, human or animal dejecta, wastewater and any other contaminated matter from a conveyance.

Article 24 of the IHR 2005 requires each ship operator to ensure that no sources of infection and contamination are found on board, including in the water system. Annex 4 requires ship operators to facilitate application of health measures and provide the health documents under the IHR 2005 (e.g. Ship Sanitation Control Exemption Certificate/ Ship Sanitation Control Certificate [also known as Ship Sanitation Certificates], Maritime Declaration of Health).

For this purpose, it is important that these measures are upheld on ships and at ports and that health measures are taken to ensure that conveyances are free from sources of infection or contamination.

1.3.2 International Labour Organization

Maritime Labour Convention, 2006

The Maritime Labour Convention, 2006,[1] adopted by the 94th (Maritime) Session of the International Labour Conference, the main body of the ILO, consolidates more than 60 existing ILO maritime labour standards, adopted by the ILO since 1919, several of which address issues relevant to health on board ships. Article IV, Seafarers' Employment and Social Rights, of the Maritime Labour Convention, 2006 provides, in paragraph 3, that "Every

[1] http://www.ilo.org/global/standards/maritime-labour-convention/lang--en/index.htm (accessed 30 January 2011).

seafarer has a right to decent working and living conditions on board ship" and, in paragraph 4, that "Every seafarer has a right to health protection, medical care, welfare measures and other forms of social protection". The following regulations of the convention specifically address health issues:

- *Regulation 1.2: Medical certificate*, paragraph 1, provides that "Seafarers shall not work on a ship unless they are certified as medically fit to perform their duties". The related mandatory standard sets out the requirements related to the medical examination of seafarers and the issuing of a medical certificate attesting that they are medically fit to perform the duties they are to carry out at sea.
- *Regulation 3.1: Accommodation and recreational facilities*, paragraph 1, provides that "Each Member shall ensure that ships that fly its flag provide and maintain decent accommodations and recreational facilities for seafarers working or living on board, or both, consistent with promoting the seafarers' health and well-being". It sets out specific requirements concerning the size of rooms and other accommodation spaces, heating and ventilation, noise and vibration, sanitary facilities, lighting and hospital accommodation. *Standard A3.1*, paragraph 18, provides that "The competent authority shall require frequent inspections to be carried out on board ships, by or under the authority of the master, to ensure that seafarer accommodation is clean, decently habitable and maintained in a good state of repair. The results of each such inspection shall be recorded and be available for review". (The competent authority is the one under the ILO.)
- *Regulation 3.2: Food and catering*, paragraph 1, provides that "Each Member shall ensure that ships that fly its flag carry on board and serve food and drinking water of appropriate quality, nutritional value and quantity that adequately covers the requirements of the ship and takes into account the differing cultural and religious backgrounds". *Standard A3.2* provides, inter alia, that "Each Member shall ensure that ships that fly its flag meet the following minimum standards: ... (b) the organization and equipment of the catering department shall be such as to permit the provision to the seafarers of adequate, varied and nutritious meals prepared and served in hygienic conditions; and (c) catering staff shall be properly trained or instructed for their positions". There are further requirements and guidance related to proper food handling and hygiene.

- *Regulation 4.1: Medical care on board ship and ashore* provides, in paragraph 1, that "Each Member shall ensure that all seafarers on ships that fly its flag are covered by adequate measures for the protection of their health and that they have access to prompt and adequate medical care whilst working on board"; in paragraph 3, that "Each Member shall ensure that seafarers on board ships in its territory who are in need of immediate medical care are given access to the Member's medical facilities on shore"; and, in paragraph 4, that "The requirements for on-board health protection and medical care set out in the Code include standards for measures aimed at providing seafarers with health protection and medical care as comparable as possible to that which is generally available to workers ashore".

Furthermore, *Regulation 5.1: Flag State responsibilities*, paragraph 1, provides that "Each Member is responsible for ensuring implementation of its obligations under this Convention on ships that fly its flag"; and paragraph 2 provides that "Each Member shall establish an effective system for the inspection and certification of maritime labour conditions ... ensuring that the working and living conditions for seafarers on ships that fly its flag meet, and continue to meet, the standards in this Convention". *Regulation 5.1.3: Maritime labour certificate and declaration of maritime labour compliance* provides, in paragraph 3, that (for ships of 500 gross tonnage and above) "Each Member shall require ships that fly its flag to carry and maintain a maritime labour certificate certifying that the working and living conditions of seafarers on the ship, including measures for ongoing compliance to be included in the declaration of maritime labour compliance ... have been inspected and meet the requirements of national laws or regulations or other measures implementing this Convention"; and, in paragraph 4, that "Each Member shall require ships that fly its flag to carry and maintain a declaration of maritime labour compliance stating the national requirements implementing this Convention for the working and living conditions for seafarers and setting out the measures adopted by the shipowner to ensure compliance with the requirements on the ship or ships concerned". The flag State, or a recognized organization that has the delegated authority to do so, is required to inspect, among other things, accommodation, food and catering and onboard medical care before issuing the certificate, which is valid for a period that shall not exceed five years (interim and intermediate certificates are also prescribed).

Work in Fishing Convention, 2007 (No. 188)[1] *and Work in Fishing Recommendation, 2007 (No. 199)*[2]

These instruments apply to fishers and fishing vessels and set out requirements and guidance on the issues of medical examination and certification of fishers, accommodation (including requirements aimed at ensuring vessels are constructed to be both safe and healthy) and food on board fishing vessels, medical care at sea, and access to medical care ashore. Annex III of the convention, paragraph 83, provides that "For vessels of 24 metres in length and over, the competent authority [under ILO] shall require frequent inspections to be carried out, by or under the authority of the skipper, to ensure that: (a) accommodation is clean, decently habitable and safe, and is maintained in a good state of repair; (b) food and water supplies are sufficient; and (c) galley and food storage spaces and equipment are hygienic and in a proper state of repair" and that "The results of such inspections, and the actions taken to address any deficiencies found, shall be recorded and available for review".

Consideration of the ILO standards

It is highly recommended that those involved in the design, construction, operation and inspection of ships, including port health officials, become fully aware of the provisions of the Maritime Labour Convention, 2006, the Work in Fishing Convention, 2007 and the Work in Fishing Recommendation, 2007, as these standards are the basis for flag and port State control of living and working conditions of merchant ships and fishing vessels.

1.3.3 International Maritime Organization

The International Maritime Organization (IMO) is a specialized agency of the United Nations, which is based in the United Kingdom, with around 300 international staff. The convention establishing the IMO was adopted in Geneva in 1948, and the IMO first met in 1959. The IMO's main task has been to develop and maintain a comprehensive regulatory framework for shipping, and its remit today includes safety, environmental concerns, legal matters, technical cooperation, maritime security and the efficiency of shipping.[3]

1 http://www.ilo.org/ilolex/cgi-lex/convde.pl?C188 (accessed 30 January 2011).

2 http://www.ilo.org/ilolex/cgi-lex/convde.pl?R199 (accessed 30 January 2011).

3 http://www.imo.org.

1.4 Roles and responsibilities

Infectious diseases on board may have a considerable toll on the operational capacity of ships and in extreme circumstances become impediments to international commerce and travel. Prevention of such incidents and a proper response should they occur are a top priority for all those responsible for ship design, construction and operation.

There are distinct roles for different organizations and individuals in maintaining good sanitation on ships. However, the objective of good ship sanitation is a common one that requires all to play their part. From design through construction, procurement, operation and docking, all professionals involved in shipping have an important role to play within the preventive risk management approach to protecting passengers, crew, port populations and international communities from harm.

The major roles of accountability on board that relate to maintaining a safe environment for passengers and crew are assigned to the owner, operator, engineer, master and medical personnel. These roles and responsibilities are briefly outlined below.

1.4.1 Designer/constructor

Good sanitary design greatly reduces the chances of poor health outcomes arising on board or when the ship is in contact with external risks at port. Therefore, those who design and construct ships need to ensure that their ships can be readily operated in a sanitary manner.

The construction and layout of the ship must be suitable for its intended purposes. This requires attention to important details of design and construction that affect ship sanitation. The better and more failsafe a ship's sanitary design, the easier it is for the owner/operator to minimize the inherent risk. In contrast, a ship's design that has many flaws and places excessive reliance on operational practices is likely to lead to disease outbreaks.

In general, design and construction of ships and associated equipment should meet internationally accepted standards (e.g. various IMO, Codex Alimentarius Commission and International Organization for Standardization standards).

1.4.2 Owner/operator

Upon receiving a ship, the owner should ensure compliance with sanitary design standards that support sanitary ship operation. Examples include the physical separation of clean food and water from waste, and adequate design capacities for facilities such as recreational water environments. Responsibility for ensuring that a ship received is designed and built in a manner that does not expose passengers and crew to unacceptable health risks rests with the ship owner. The owner bears ongoing responsibility for ensuring that the ship design is fit for its intended purpose.

Responsibility for ensuring that the ship can be operated in a manner that provides a safe environment for passengers and crew rests with the ship operator. The operator must ensure that there are adequate and properly maintained equipment and provisions, with sufficient numbers of adequately trained crew to properly manage health risks on board.

1.4.3 Master/crew

According to the IMO's International Management Code for the Safe Operation of Ships and for Pollution Prevention,[1] the ultimate responsibility for all aspects of crew safety on board is vested with the ship's master, as delegated by the operator. Responsibilities are often delegated such that they effectively become shared, although not abrogated, via the chain of command. The master must ensure that all reasonable measures are taken to protect crew and passenger health. Conscientious and diligent monitoring of operational control measures is the responsibility of the master and crew.

The ship's engineer is likely to be chiefly responsible, as delegated by the master, for the proper operation of the engineered systems that protect passengers and crew. These include many aspects of the ship's operation, such as the cooling and heating systems designed to maintain food and water at safe temperatures, water treatment systems for drinking-water, waste management and the integrity of piping and storage systems.

1.4.4 Port authorities

A responsibility of port authorities is to provide the required equipment, facilities, expertise and materials so that ships can undertake operations (e.g. providing safe food and water, safely removing ballast and waste) in a sanitary manner. One or more agencies may fulfil the roles of the port authority, health authority and competent authority of a flag State under the IMO.

---

[1] http://www.imo.org/OurWork/HumanElement/SafetyManagement/Pages/ISMCode.aspx (accessed 30 January 2011).

Prevention of contamination at source to the maximum degree practicable is a key tenet of preventive control strategies. As ships load at ports, the port authorities play a vital role in protecting public health by seeking to provide the best practicable raw materials for ships. Authorities should clarify which entity has the Ship Sanitation Certificate and food inspection responsibilities.

1.5 Structure of the *Guide to ship sanitation*

This guide is structured into the following chapters:

- Chapter 1. Introduction
- Chapter 2. Water
- Chapter 3. Food
- Chapter 4. Recreational water environments
- Chapter 5. Ballast water
- Chapter 6. Waste management and disposal
- Chapter 7. Vector and reservoir control
- Chapter 8. Controlling infectious disease agents in the environment.

Chapter 1 sets the guide in its legal context, considering the IHR 2005 and describing its relationship to other international documents, regulations and standards.

Each of chapters 2–8 follows the same structural approach and consists of two sections: background and guidelines.

The background section describes critical issues and supporting health evidence applicable to ships and the specific topic of the chapter.

The guidelines section provides user-targeted information and guidance applicable to the topic of the chapter, identifying responsibilities and providing examples of practices that should control risks. This section contains a number of specific *guidelines* (a situation to aim for and maintain), each of which is accompanied by a set of *indicators* (measures for whether the guidelines are met) and *guidance notes* (advice on applying the guidelines and indicators in practice, highlighting the most important aspects that need to be considered when setting priorities for action).

2 Water

2.1 Background

Improperly managed water is an established route for infectious disease transmission on ships. The importance of water was illustrated in the review of more than 100 outbreaks associated with ships undertaken by Rooney et al. (2004), in which one fifth were attributed to a waterborne route. This is probably an underestimate, as more than one third of the 100 reviewed outbreaks could not be associated with any specific exposure route, so some may have been waterborne. Furthermore, water may be a source of primary or index cases of a disease that might then be transmitted via other routes.

Most waterborne outbreaks of disease on ships involve ingestion of water contaminated with pathogens derived from human or other animal excreta. Illnesses due to chemical poisoning of water have also occurred on ships, although chemical incidents are much less commonly reported than microbial ones.

To protect the health of passengers and crew, water used for potable purposes on board ship should be provided with sanitary safeguards in a multiple-barrier system (from the shore and distribution system, including connections to the ship system, through the ship treatment and storage systems and on to each water supply outlet), in order to prevent contamination or pollution during ship operation.

Waterborne outbreaks have been associated with bunkering water of poor quality. Therefore, the first strategy for prevention of waterborne disease should be to load ships with water that conforms to the WHO *Guidelines for drinking-water quality* (GDWQ) (WHO, 2011) or relevant national standards, whichever are stricter.

Even if the water at the port is safe, this does not ensure that it will remain safe during the transfer and storage activities that follow. An understanding of the ship drinking-water supply and transfer chain will help to illustrate the points at which the water can become contaminated en route to the taps on board.

Generally, the ship drinking-water supply and transfer chain consists of three major components (Figure 2-1):

1. the source of water coming into the port;

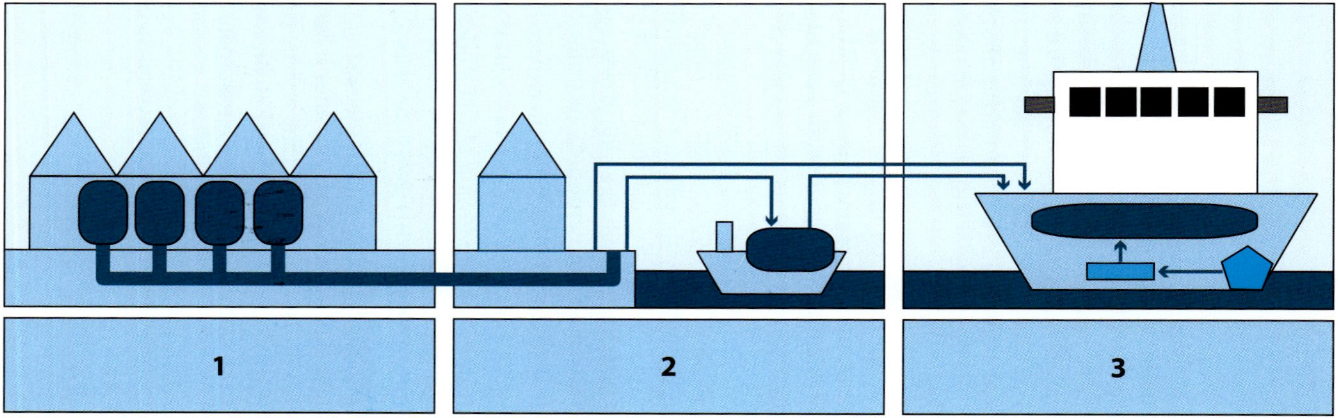

Figure 2-1 Schematic of ship drinking-water supply chain, showing 1) source, 2) transfer and delivery system and 3) ship water system

2. the transfer and delivery system, which includes hydrants, hoses, water boats and water barges; this water transfer process provides multiple opportunities for the introduction of contaminants into the drinking-water;
3. the ship water system, which includes storage, distribution and onboard production of drinking-water from overboard sources, such as seawater.

2.1.1 Standards related to potable water

The GDWQ (WHO, 2011) describe reasonable minimum requirements for safe practices to protect the health of consumers and derive numerical guideline values for constituents of water or indicators of water quality. Neither the minimum requirements for safe practices nor the numerical guideline values are mandatory limits, but rather health-based guidance to national authorities to help them establish their own enforceable standards, which may also consider other factors. In order to define such limits, it is necessary to consider the GDWQ in the context of local or national environmental, social, economic and cultural conditions. Nevertheless, given the global nature of ship travel and the need for ships to board water from areas with variable and possibly inadequate standards of general hygiene and sanitation, the GDWQ (or national standards, if more stringent) should be followed. This approach will provide passengers and crew with consistent, reliable protection from the potential risks posed by contaminated drinking-water.

The GDWQ provide comprehensive guidance to ensure the quality and safety of drinking-water. Microbial risks in water on board ships are the principal concerns, although a few risks associated with toxic chemicals also exist.

The WHO *Guidelines for Drinking-water Quality* (WHO, 2011) (GDWQ) identify the broad spectrum of contaminants, including microorganisms, inorganic and synthetic organic chemicals, disinfection by-products and radionuclides, that can reach hazardous concentrations in potable water supplies and describe systematic approaches to risk management. Safe drinking-water, as defined by the GDWQ, does not represent any significant risk to health over a lifetime of consumption, including different sensitivities that may occur between life stages.

ILO Convention C133 (Accommodation of Crews [Supplementary Provisions] Convention, 1970[1]) defines minimum standards for provision of potable water for crews and has been ratified by many States.

[1] http://www.ilo.org/ilolex/cgi-lex/convde.pl?C133 (accessed 30 January 2011).

The Maritime Labour Convention, 2006 provides comprehensive rights and protections at work for seafarers. The new labour standard consolidates and updates more than 65 international labour standards related to seafarers adopted over the past 80 years. Regulation 3.2 of the Maritime Labour Convention, 2006 includes requirements for drinking-water on board.

In the IMO's Life-Saving Appliance Code (IMO, 2010), additional information about potable water requirements in rescue boats is provided.

Reference can be made to seven international standards in relation to sanitary design and construction of ship water supplies and potable water quality assessment:[1]

1. ISO 15748-1:2002—Ships and marine technology—Potable water supply on ships and marine structures—Part 1: Planning and design;
2. ISO 15748-2:2002—Ships and marine technology—Potable water supply on ships and marine structures—Part 2: Method of calculation;
3. ISO 19458:2006—Water quality—Sampling for microbiological analysis;
4. ISO 14726:2008—Ships and marine technology—Identification colours for the content of piping systems;
5. ISO/IEC 17025:2005—General requirements for the competence of testing and calibration laboratories;
6. ISO 5620-1:1992—Shipbuilding and marine structures—Filling connection for drinking water tanks—Part 1: General requirements;
7. ISO 5620-2:1992—Shipbuilding and marine structures—Filling connection for drinking water tanks—Part 2: Components.

2.1.2 Role of the International Health Regulations (2005)

The IHR 2005 contain provisions for the State Party to designate ports to develop core capacities, such as the capacity to ensure a safe environment for travellers using port facilities, including potable water supplies (Annex 1B1(d) of the IHR 2005).

In accordance with Articles 22(b), 22(e) and 24(c) of the IHR 2005, Member States are required to take all practicable measures to ensure that international conveyance operators keep their conveyances free

[1] http://www.iso.org.

from sources of contamination and infection, and competent authorities are responsible for ensuring that the facilities at international ports are in sanitary condition and for supervising the removal and safe disposal of any contaminated water and food from a conveyance.

However, it is the responsibility of each ship operator to establish all practicable measures to ensure that no sources of infection or contamination are present on board, including in the water system. For this purpose, it is important that regulations and standards are upheld on board ships and at ports, in terms of the safety of food and water served on board, from the source of supply ashore to distribution on board ship.

2.1.3 Potable water sources from ashore and uses on board ships

A port may receive potable water from either a municipal or a private supply and usually has special arrangements for managing this water after it has entered the port.

Potable water is used in various ways on board ships, including direct human consumption, food preparation and sanitation/hygiene activities. Potential uses include:

- preparation of hot and cold beverages, such as coffee, tea and powdered beverages;
- ice cubes in drinks;
- reconstitution of dehydrated foods, such as soups, noodles and infant formula;
- food washing and preparation;
- direct ingestion from cold-water taps and water fountains;
- reconstitution and/or ingestion of medications;
- brushing of teeth;
- hand and face washing, bathing and showering;
- dishwashing, and cleaning of utensils and work areas;
- laundering purposes (could potentially use a lower grade of water);
- emergency medical use.

Although some uses do not necessitate consumption, they involve human contact and possibly incidental ingestion (e.g. tooth brushing).

Although, whenever practicable, it is useful to have only one water system installed to supply potable water for drinking, culinary, dishwashing, ablutionary and laundering purposes, two or three systems are sometimes installed or required: potable, sanitary and wash water, for example. A wash-water system can be used to supply slop sinks, laundry facilities, water closets, bibcock connections for deck flushing and cleaning purposes, heated water for dishwashing and water for other special uses. All non-potable water taps need to be labelled with words such as "UNFIT FOR DRINKING". There should never be a connection between wash-water or other non-potable systems and the potable water system without using an appropriate backflow-prevention device.

2.1.4 Health risks associated with potable water on ships

Some of the causal hazardous agents associated with waterborne disease outbreaks on board ships are listed in Table 2-1. Note that in some waterborne disease outbreaks, the causative agent was not identified. Outbreaks were associated with such causes as:

- contaminated water supplied at the port
- contaminated bunkered water
- cross-connections between potable and non-potable water
- poor design and construction of potable water storage tanks
- inadequate disinfection.

Some ports were found not to have supplied a safe source of water. In these cases, contaminated water bunkered from port was associated with a number of outbreaks due to enterotoxigenic *Escherichia coli*, *Giardia lamblia* and *Cryptosporidium*.

Table 2-1 Pathogens and toxins linked to outbreaks of waterborne disease associated with ships, 1 January 1970 – 30 June 2003

Pathogen/toxin	Number of outbreaks	Number of passengers and crew members affected
Enterotoxigenic *Escherichia coli*	7	2917
Norovirus	3	788
Salmonella typhi	1	83
Salmonella spp.	1	292
Shigella spp.	1	690
Cryptosporidium spp.	1	42
Giardia lamblia	1	200
Unknown agent	5	849
Chemical water poisoning	1	544
Total	**21**	**6405**

Source: Rooney et al. (2004).

Space is often very limited on ships. Potable water systems are likely to be physically close to hazardous substances, such as sewage or waste streams, increasing the chance of cross-connections. Cold-water systems may be close to sources of heat, and this elevated temperature increases the risk of proliferation of *Legionella* spp. and the growth of other microbial life.

In considering evidence from outbreaks, the presence of pathogens generally transmitted to humans from other human sources (e.g. viral pathogens and *Shigella* spp.) indicates that contamination with sewage is one of the more common causes of waterborne disease outbreaks on ships.

Legionnaires' disease is perhaps the most widely known form of legionellosis. It is a form of pneumonia acquired from inhaling aerosols of water that contain excessive numbers of *Legionella* bacteria. Ships are considered high-risk environments for the proliferation of *Legionella* spp. for a variety of reasons. Firstly, source water quality could potentially be a health concern if untreated or subject only to treatment with a residual disinfectant prior to or upon bunkering. Secondly, water storage and distribution systems on ships are complex and could provide greater opportunities for bacterial contamination, as ship movement increases the risk of surge and back-siphonage. Thirdly, potable water may vary in temperature (e.g. due to high temperatures in the engine room). In some tropical regions, the risks of bacterial growth and occurrence of *Legionella* contamination in cold-water systems are greater because of higher water temperatures. Finally, proliferation is encouraged due to long-term storage and stagnation in tanks or pipes. Importantly, *Legionella* spp. can proliferate in warm-water temperatures between 25 °C and 50 °C, such as those experienced in showerheads and spa pools, leading to potential exposure through aerosolization arising from showers and other plumbing fixtures. Many cases of Legionnaires' disease associated with ships are linked to whirlpool spas (WHO, 2001; see also chapter 4). *Legionella pneumophila* has been found in drinking-water systems on general cargo ships (Temeshnikova et al., 1996).

The production of water on ships can be associated with its own potential health problems. Ships can produce their own water by several different processes, such as reverse osmosis or evaporation of seawater. Desalination demineralizes seawater, which can make it more corrosive, shortening the life of containers and conduits. Desalinated water may also cause health impacts associated with insufficient minerals in seafarers' diets or the consumption of dissolved metals (e.g. lead, nickel, iron, cadmium or copper) from corrosion products. Desalinated water may also be considered bland, flavourless and unacceptable by passengers and crew.

Evaporation systems on board ships are supplied with seawater that has been sucked in through so-called sea chests and is typically led directly into the evaporator. In the evaporator, the seawater that is heated by the engine cooling water typically starts boiling at low temperatures (<80 °C), due to low pressure within these systems. When these low process temperatures are used, there is no guarantee of producing water free from pathogens. According to International Organization for Standardization (ISO) standards, water that has been produced below 80 °C needs to be disinfected before it can be defined as potable water. The emerging steam condenses as distillate inside the evaporator. This distillate is collected and flows to further treatment components. It should be considered that the distillate is free from any minerals and almost free from carbon dioxide. As a result, it is necessary to add carbon dioxide to the distilled water to prepare it for the rehardening process.

Reverse osmosis involves pretreatment and transport of water across membranes under pressure so that salts are excluded. Post-treatment may also occur before distribution. Partial desalination or breaches in membranes may have potential health implications due to trace elements and organic compounds, including oil and refined petroleum products, occurring within the source seawater. In addition, seawater sources may contain hazards not encountered in freshwater systems. These include diverse harmful algae and cyanobacteria, certain free-living bacteria (including *Vibrio* species such as *V. parahaemolyticus* and *V. cholerae*) and some chemicals, such as boron and bromide, which are more abundant in seawater.

Repair work on a treatment and distribution system can offer several opportunities for widespread contamination of water supplies. Ship operators should take special precautions when carrying out repairs to storage tanks. For example, an outbreak of typhoid on a ship occurred after the potable water was contaminated with sewage while the ship underwent repairs in dry dock. Good hygienic practice and post-repair cleaning and disinfection are necessary. Ship builders and rehabilitators typically have written procedures for physical cleaning and disinfection before commissioning or recommissioning ships.

2.1.5 Bottled water and ice

Bottled water is considered as drinking-water by some regulatory agencies and as a food by others (WHO, 2011). International quality specifications for bottled water exist under the Codex Alimentarius Commission (FAO/WHO, 2001) and are derived from the GDWQ (WHO, 2011). As it is commonly designated as a food product, bottled water is considered in chapter 3 on food.

Within this guide, ice supplied to ships or manufactured on board for both drinking and cooling is classified as food. Guidance pertaining to ice used on ships is contained in chapter 3. The GDWQ (WHO, 2011) apply to both packaged water and ice intended for human consumption.

2.1.6 Definitions, overview and objectives of water safety plans

Water safety plans (WSPs) are an effective overarching management approach for ensuring the safety of a drinking-water supply. WSPs are equivalent to food safety plans or programmes, incorporating hazard analysis and critical control points, implemented as part of food safety management (see chapter 3). As discussed above, a potable water source at the port is not a guarantee of safe water on board, because water may become contaminated during transfer to the ship or during storage or distribution on board. A WSP covering water management within ports, from receipt of water through to its transfer to the ship, complemented by water quality measures on board, provides a framework for water safety on ships. A general overview of WSPs follows; their specific application to the safety of drinking-water on board ships is described in section 2.2.

A WSP has three key components, guided by health-based targets and overseen through drinking-water supply chain surveillance. They are:

- system assessments, which include
  - description of the water supply system in order to determine whether the drinking-water supply chain (up to the point of consumption) as a whole can deliver water of a quality that meets health-based targets;
  - identification of hazards and evaluation of risks;
  - determination of control measures, reassessment and prioritization of risks;
  - development, implementation and maintenance of an improvement plan;
- operational monitoring, which includes identification and monitoring of the control measures that will ensure that management processes are functioning efficiently;
- management and communication, including verification, preparation of management procedures and development of supporting programmes to manage people and processes, including upgrade and improvement.

The various steps involved in designing and implementing a WSP are illustrated in Figure 2-2. For more information on general principles of WSPs, see the GDWQ (WHO, 2011) and the *Water safety plan manual* (Bartram et al., 2009).

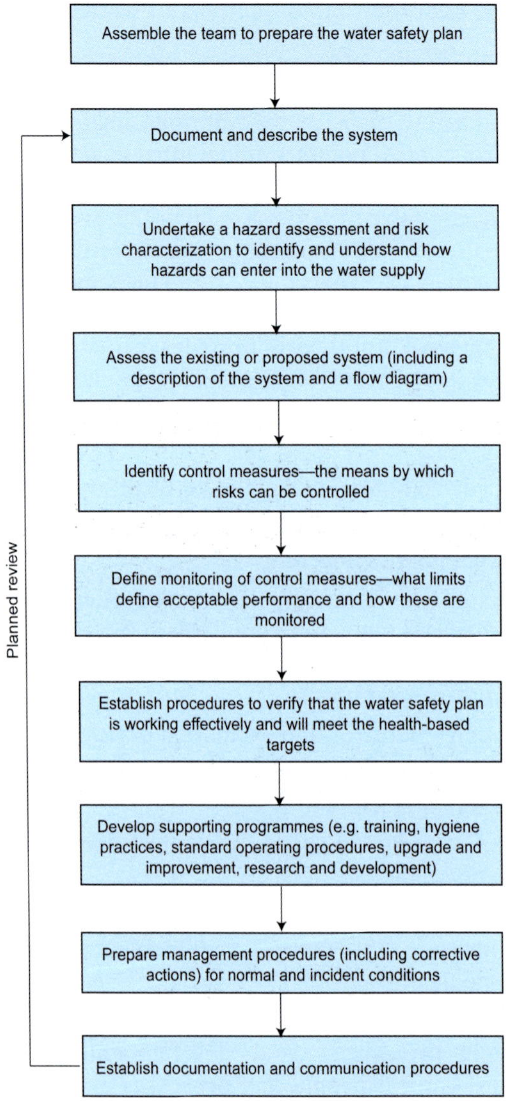

Figure 2-2 Application of water safety plans

2.2 Guidelines

2.2.1 Guideline 2.1: Water safety plan for shore supplies, delivery system and bunker boats or barges

Guideline 2.1—A water safety plan has been designed and implemented for the port water source, for the bunker boats or barges and for the delivery system to the ship.

Indicators for Guideline 2.1

1. A potable water system assessment has been carried out, with risks and control points identified.
2. Operational monitoring, including operational limits and target criteria, has been defined for the port water system and bunker boats or barges, and corrective action plans have been developed.
3. Management systems, including record keeping, validation, verification and communication, have been included in the WSP of the port water system and bunker boats or barges.

Guidance notes for Guideline 2.1

The GDWQ are intended to cover a broad range of water supplies and are not specifically targeted at ships. Therefore, in drawing from the guidance provided in the GDWQ, the specific context of the port and the ship needs to be taken into consideration. The overall approach promoted, involving the development and implementation of a WSP (Bartram et al., 2009; WHO, 2011), is as relevant to ships and ports as it is to any other water supply situation.

Roles and responsibilities

A WSP is an effective means of achieving consistency in ensuring the safety of a drinking-water supply. The entity responsible for each component of the drinking-water supply chain (i.e. port water source, shore water distribution system, transfer and delivery system and ship water system) should be responsible for the preparation and implementation of a WSP for that part of the process. Examples of roles and responsibilities for each component are as follows:

- *Source water supplier (public or private)*: Role is to provide to the port a safe water supply of sufficient quantity and quality. Responsibilities are to monitor the water system by sampling water and providing sampling results to the port authority on request, informing the port authority of any adverse results and actions to be taken, with the obligation to inform the port authority when the water supply has, or may, become contaminated. This is typically the municipal water supplier for the area in which the port is located.

- *Port operator and water supplier*: Role is to maintain the integrity of water supplied throughout the shore water distribution system and to provide safe water to the ship. Responsibilities are to maintain a safe water supply from the shore water distribution system through delivery to the ship; to monitor the water system and share sampling results with the source water supplier, authorities and appropriate stakeholders; and to take corrective action as necessary.

1. System assessment for port water system, water boats and barges and delivery to the ship

Potable water for ships, including water boats and barges, needs to be obtained only from those water sources and supplies that provide potable water of a quality that meets the standards recommended in the GDWQ (WHO, 2011) or national standards, whichever are stricter. Particular attention should be paid to microbial water quality, although physical and chemical requirements are also important.

Water is delivered to ships by hoses on the dockside or transferred to the ship by water boats or barges. Designated filling hoses must be provided at each pier or wharf for the use of ships not equipped with them. Facilities for the direct delivery of water from shore sources to the filling line for the ship's potable water system include piping, hydrants, hoses and any other necessary equipment.

Plans for the construction or replacement of facilities for bunkering potable water on board must be submitted to the competent authority under the IHR 2005 for review. Plans must show the location and size of the distribution lines, location and type of check valves or backflow preventers, location and type of hydrants, including details of outlet protection, and storage lockers for filling hoses and attachments.

In some instances, local source water may be contaminated with protozoan pathogens (e.g. *Cryptosporidium*) or viruses, whose presence may not be well indicated by *E. coli* or thermotolerant (faecal) coliforms, and which require more stringent treatment. Based on the findings of the WSP, additional controls and measurements may be necessary. Some disinfectants are effective at inactivating *E. coli*, but not *Cryptosporidium* or viruses. For instance, typical doses of chlorine or chloramine are ineffective against *Cryptosporidium*, so membrane filtration or ultraviolet (UV) disinfection might need to be used; commonly used doses of UV disinfection are of limited value in controlling viruses, so higher UV doses or free chlorine may need to be used.

Disinfection

The water supply delivered to ports must be suitable for distribution and consumption without further treatment, except as necessary to maintain water quality in the distribution system (e.g. supplemental disinfection, addition of corrosion-control chemicals). A disinfectant residual should be detectable in water samples at the port, on the water barge and on the ship. Presence of a measurable disinfectant residual contributes to ensuring that water is microbiologically safe for the intended use. Presence of the residual will be affected by the original dose of disinfectant, type of disinfectant used, disinfectant demand, temperature and pH of the water and time since application. A significant reduction in disinfectant residual may also indicate post-treatment contamination.

New or repaired facilities must be disinfected before they are returned to service.

In the event of contamination of the water provided to the port, the port must complete corrective action and notify the party responsible for bunkering water as soon as possible to enable mitigation to prevent contaminated water from being transported onto ships.

Prevention of backflow and cross-contamination

The lines' capacity should maintain positive pressure at all times to reduce the risk of backflow. There must be no connections between the potable water system and other piping systems. All fittings, meters and other appurtenances used for bunkering of potable water need to be handled and stored in a sanitary manner. Inlets and outlets of potable water meters are typically capped when not in use.

Approved backflow preventers need to be properly installed between the ship and shore systems to permit effective operation and inspection. Drainage to prevent freezing may be needed.

Non-potable water hydrants are not normally located on the same pier as hydrants for potable water unless absolutely necessary. Potable water hydrants must be identified with signs such as "POTABLE WATER", and non-potable water hydrants with signs marked "NON-POTABLE WATER". Hydrants need to be adequately covered and located so as not to receive waste discharge from ships. Drainage lines from supply lines or hydrants (or taps and faucets) should terminate above normal high-water level or the surge of water from incoming ships. Where compressed air is used to blow water out of lines and hydrants, a filter, liquid trap or similar device must be installed in the supply line from the compressed air system to protect the water supply.

Water boats and barges

Water boats and barges are ships especially constructed and equipped to receive and provide water for both potable and non-potable water systems on board ships when direct shore delivery is not practicable. These boats have water tanks, water hoses and fittings, pumps and independent pipe systems to provide potable water to onboard systems.

Reception, handling, storage and delivery to ship water systems need to be carried out under controlled, sanitary conditions. All hoses, fittings and tools need to be stored in designated lockers that are closed and clean. Operators need to possess knowledge of water hygiene and good sanitary practice.

Facilities for disinfection, when and where necessary on board, need to be available. Regular cleaning and disinfection of hoses and fittings should be performed. Plans for construction of ships must show filling lines, storage tanks, pumping equipment and protective measures for approval by the port health authority or other designated authority.

In the event of contamination of potable water at the delivery point or on the water boat or barge, the party responsible for transfer of the water must complete corrective action and notify the ship's operator as soon as possible so that they can take mitigative measures to prevent contaminated water from being transported onto the ship.

3. Monitoring and verification

By far the greatest risks associated with drinking-water involve microbial contamination from human excreta. Source water is monitored at the port to ensure that water is safe. Recommended parameters to be monitored include *E. coli* or thermotolerant (faecal) coliforms, disinfectant residual, corrosion-related contaminants, turbidity, heterotrophic plate count (HPC) and aesthetic parameters. *Escherichia coli* or thermotolerant (faecal) coliforms are used as the indicators of potential contamination from pathogens associated with human excreta. Total coliforms are not necessarily indicators of faecal contamination, but may reflect a lack of general cleanliness. *Escherichia coli* and thermotolerant (faecal) coliforms should be measured using generally accepted analytical techniques. HPC should be measured to provide an overview of the general status of microbial life in the system.

Faecal indicators such as *E. coli* or thermotolerant (faecal) coliforms are valuable for ongoing verification or for batch testing of water that is on hold, but are of limited use for operational monitoring of water supplied on the ship, as even very brief exposure to unsafe water can lead to an outbreak. The tests typically take 18–24 hours to report, by which time water may have been consumed. No *E. coli* or thermotolerant (faecal) coliforms should be detected in any 100 ml sample of the water. A positive test may indicate potential pathogenic (primarily bacterial) microorganisms associated with excreta, suggesting recent or substantial post-treatment faecal contamination or inadequate treatment.

It is important to check turbidity levels of the source water, as high levels of turbidity can protect microorganisms from disinfection, stimulate growth of bacteria and cause a significant disinfectant demand. In case of high turbidity, filtration can help to solve an acute problem, but the reason for high turbidity should be identified to avoid further problems.

Provided that water entering the port conforms to acceptable standards, the principal concern regarding chemical contamination is likely to be metals leaching from the shore water distribution system. Corrosion in plumbing systems is a function of the stability and aggressiveness of the water towards the surfaces and fixtures with which the water will be in contact during transport and storage. Metals such as lead, nickel, iron, cadmium and copper can be leached from some materials into the water and may adversely affect taste or, in some cases, lead to health concerns. The need to monitor other chemicals of concern should be determined, depending on the local situation. All samples should meet GDWQ or national standards for chemicals, as there are potentially significant effects associated with chronic exposures.

Documentation of monitoring should be kept for assurance and analysis in the event of an incident.

2.2.2 Guideline 2.2: Water quantity

Guideline 2.2—Potable water is available in sufficient quantities.

Indicators for Guideline 2.2

1. Potable water quantities at the port are sufficient to ensure adequate pressure at all taps to minimize the potential for contamination.

2. Potable water quantities on board are sufficient to meet foreseeable needs for all purposes (e.g. drinking, food preparation, sanitation and hygiene activities) and to achieve sufficient water pressure at each tap to minimize the potential for contamination.

Guidance notes for Guideline 2.2

In providing adequate storage for potable water, consideration needs to be given to the size of the ship's complement of officers and crew, the maximum number of passengers accommodated, the time and distance between ports with potable water sources and the availability of water suitable for treatment on board. Sufficient storage is needed to preclude the need for treating overboard water from heavily contaminated areas and to allow time for maintenance and repair.

The amount of storage may be decreased if the potable water supply can be supplemented by water produced on board to adequate safety standards.

An insufficient or non-existent quantity of potable water under pressure on board for drinking, culinary purposes and personal hygiene can have an impact on the health and welfare of passengers and crew. However, the amount of water required for these purposes should be adequately dealt with in typical ship designs. In no case should potable water storage be less than a reasonable base level that would allow water to be supplied during maintenance or repair of treatment systems, typically a two-day supply.

2.2.3 Guideline 2.3: Water safety plan for ship water supply

Guideline 2.3—A water safety plan has been designed and implemented for the ship water system.

Indicators for Guideline 2.3

1. A potable water system assessment has been carried out, with risks and control points identified.
2. Operational monitoring, including operational limits and health-related targets, has been defined for the ship's water supply system, and corrective action plans have been developed, where necessary.
3. Management systems, including documentation, validation, verification and communication, have been included in the ship WSP.

Examples of hazards, control measures, monitoring procedures and corrective actions taken as part of a WSP for a ship water supply system are given in the Annex.

Guidance notes for Guideline 2.3

Roles and responsibilities of ship operator

The ship operator's role is to provide a safe water supply to passengers and crew, fit for all intended purposes. Water on board should be kept clean and free from pathogenic organisms and harmful chemicals. Responsibilities are to monitor the water system, particularly for microbial and chemical indicators, to share sampling results with stakeholders, to report adverse results to the competent authority under the IHR 2005, where required, and to take corrective action. Adverse results should also be communicated to the crew and passengers when and where necessary. Where there are methods or materials recommended by WHO for particular tests, these should be applied.

The ship's master or officer responsible for bunkering water must be responsible for ascertaining whether or not the source of the water is potable. All staff should be encouraged to report symptoms indicating a potential waterborne disease. The ship's operator needs to provide adequate toilet and washing facilities for the crew to maintain personal hygiene. Known carriers of communicable diseases should never come into contact with potable water supplies. An adequate ratio of crew to facilities is required on board ship to enable proper servicing and maintenance activities. Minimum requirements can be found in ILO Convention C133 and the Maritime Labour Convention, 2006. The term "fresh water" used in ILO conventions and the Maritime Labour Convention, 2006 should be interpreted as meaning potable water. To reduce disease spread among crew, shared drinking receptacles should not be used on ships unless they are sanitized between uses.

1. Assessment of the ship's potable water system: hazards and hazardous events

The ship operator should be aware of all hazards (biological, chemical or physical) and hazardous events that may occur in port water when transferring water from port to ship or when water is produced, stored and distributed on board. All potential hazards and hazardous events should be assessed within the WSP. Knowledge of these hazards may be obtained from various sources, including data on water quality from the port health authority and epidemiological data on waterborne disease in the region of concern.

Outbreaks of illness due to toxic chemicals are much less frequent than those due to microbial hazards. Nevertheless, passengers and crew may be exposed to chemical contaminants in drinking-water over extended periods of time. These contaminants may have been present in the source water, be introduced into the water from leaching of components within the ship water distribution system or be present in water produced on board, such as boron and bromide from improperly treated seawater. Therefore, water on board should meet the GDWQ (or national standards, if more stringent) for chemicals of concern.

Corrosion in plumbing systems is a function of the stability and aggressiveness of the water towards the surfaces and fixtures that the water will contact during transport and storage. Desalinated water produced on board ships may be corrosive, for example, and salt water and saline atmospheres may have corrosive effects on fixtures.

Source of potable water

Potable water for ships needs to be obtained only from water sources and water supplies that provide potable water of a quality in line with standards recommended in the GDWQ (WHO, 2011) or national standards, if more stringent, specifically in relation to microbial, chemical, physical and radiological requirements.

The ship's operator must seek assurance as to the quality and nature of the source water before bunkering. Ship operators may choose to directly engage with port and local authorities to investigate levels of safety. If water is suspected to come from an unsafe source, testing for contamination may be necessary. If water provided at the port does not meet the GDWQ (or national requirements, if stricter), the port will need to utilize an alternative, higher-quality source. Terminal disinfection is a treatment step and, where a residual disinfectant is required, a final safeguard.

Ships using ports where water treatment is unreliable must carry calibrated equipment for basic testing (turbidity, pH and disinfectant residual) and ensure capacity to dose disinfectant or filter to appropriate levels to provide a minimum level of safety.

Detection of undesirable aesthetic parameters (odour/colour/taste) may indicate cross-connections with the liquid waste system or other potential contamination problems and should be investigated.

Bunkering stations

To mitigate risks during bunkering of potable water, multiple-barrier protection should be established. This starts with the use of appropriate hoses and fixtures, backflow preventers and filters at the bunker station and chlorination before water enters the storage tank. To help protect the quality of water passing through filling hoses, they should be durable, with a smooth, impervious lining, and equipped with fittings that are designed to permit connection to the shore water supply system. Interior surfaces of potable water hoses should be made of material suitable for being disinfected and should not support the growth of biofilm. Hoses that are designed to be used for firefighting are not appropriate for use as potable water hoses. Potable water hoses should be clearly identifiable with words such as "POTABLE WATER". Hoses used exclusively for the delivery of potable water should be kept on each ship. The ends should be capped when not in use. Keeper chains will prevent misplacement of caps. The hose needs to be handled to prevent contamination by dragging ends on the ground, pier or deck surfaces or by dropping into the harbour water. A hose that has become contaminated should be thoroughly flushed and disinfected. The hose must be flushed in all cases before being attached to the filling line. It must be drained and dried after each use.

The filling hoses should be stowed, with the ends capped, in special lockers designated and marked "POTABLE WATER HOSE ONLY". Lockers must be closed, self-draining and fixed above the deck. The lockers should be constructed from smooth, non-toxic, corrosion-resistant and easily cleanable material. Hoses and fittings need to be maintained in good repair.

Non-potable water, if used on the ship, should be bunkered through separate piping using fittings incompatible with potable water bunkering. This water should flow through a completely different piping system that is identified with a different colour.

To provide for safe bunkering, every potable water tank must have a dedicated, clean filling line to which a hose can be attached. To avoid accidental connections of sewage hoses, the flange of this filling line should refer to suitable criteria such as defined in ISO 5620-1/2. To prevent contamination of water, the filling line needs to be positioned a suitable distance above the top of the tank or of the deck that the line penetrates. It is typically painted or marked in blue and labelled "POTABLE WATER FILLING". The filling line can have a screw cap or plug fastened by a chain to an adjacent bulkhead or surface in such a manner that the cap or plug will not touch the deck when hanging free. Lines to divert potable water to other systems by valves or interchangeable pipe fittings are not generally considered acceptable, except where an air gap follows a valve. If only one filling line is used to load potable water to all tanks, a direct connection between the potable water tank and other tanks through an air gap is a satisfactory practice. To avoid intake of unwanted particles, a filter can be used in the filling line. These filters need to be backwashed or exchanged regularly according to the manufacturer's instructions. All potable water passing through the potable water filling line should pass through an automatic chlorination unit before it enters the potable water tanks.

Water production on board

To help prevent cross-contamination, when seawater is to be treated on board for use as potable water, the overboard discharges should not be on the same side as the water intake. When it is not practicable to locate the overboard discharges on the opposite side of the ship, they should be located as far aft of, and as far below, the water intake as practicable.

Water may be produced on ships by desalination, reverse osmosis or distillation. A complete desalination process demineralizes seawater. This makes it corrosive, shortening the life of containers and conduits with which it is in contact. Special consideration needs to be given to the quality of such materials, and normal procedures for certification of materials as suitable for potable water use may not be adequate for "aggressive" desalinated water.

Because of the aggressive nature of desalinated water and because this water may be considered bland, flavourless and unacceptable, it is commonly stabilized by the addition of chemicals such as calcium carbonate. Once such treatment has been applied, desalinated waters should be no more aggressive than waters normally encountered in drinking-water supply. Chemicals used in such treatment must be subject to procedures for certification and quality assurance. The process of remineralization of desalinated water must be validated by the use of a testing kit for pH, hardness and turbidity. Water that has not been stabilized as a result of a failure in the rehardening process typically shows a very low electrical conductivity (e.g. 50 μS/cm) and an elevated pH (above 8.0). High pH can be a reason for an unsatisfactory disinfection result, and reduced hardness may lead to leaching of metals into the water.

An evaporating plant that distils seawater and supplies water to the potable water system must be of such a design to produce potable water reliably. Distillation uses heat and pressure changes to vaporize seawater, thus liberating it of its dissolved and suspended solids and almost all dissolved gases. High- and low-pressure units connected directly to the potable water lines should have the ability to go to the waste system if the distillate is not fit for use. As water is evaporated at low temperatures (<80 °C) in low-pressure units, it cannot be guaranteed that the distillate is free from pathogens. According to ISO standards, water that has been produced at temperatures below 80 °C needs to be disinfected before it can be defined as potable.

Disinfection should be implemented in the water treatment process, ideally in a way that guarantees that all water (including bunkered water) is treated before reaching the potable water tank. A distillation plant or other process that supplies water to the ship's potable water system must not operate in polluted waters or harbour areas, as some volatile pollutants may be carried through this process.

Treatment facilities should be designed to ensure efficient operation with the production of potable water that conforms to the GDWQ (WHO, 2011) or any relevant authority's requirements.

Materials

Materials used in the construction of all of the surfaces (hoses, couplings, pipes, tanks, fixtures, soldered joints) with which water may be in contact during production, transfer and storage should be approved for this purpose by an appropriate authority (regulatory or independent third party). The water that is being provided should not be corrosive to those surfaces and fixtures. Factors such as temperature, pH and alkalinity need to be controlled within appropriate ranges for the particular water type (see WHO, 2011). Concerns have emerged in relation to plasticizers, solvents, jointing compounds and coatings used in water supply and transport systems. It is important to ensure that all materials that may come in contact with the water supply are suitable and will not contribute hazardous chemicals to the water. If a pipe or tank is constructed of a material that requires coating, such coating should not lead to the water becoming toxic or otherwise unfit for human consumption (e.g. chemical odour). Materials and devices must be suitable for hot or cold water use, as applicable.

Potable water tanks

Potable water needs to be stored in tanks constructed and located so as to be protected from any contamination from inside or outside the tank. Tanks need to be designed so that cross-connections between them and tanks holding non-potable water or pipes containing non-potable water are prevented. Ideally, potable water tanks should be located in rooms that have no sources of heat emission or dirt.

Potable water tanks must be constructed of metal or other suitable material that is safe for contact with potable water, and must be robust enough to exclude contamination. Proper maintenance of anticorrosive coatings in water tanks is important. Ideally, potable water tanks would not share a common wall with the hull or other tanks containing non-potable liquids. No drainage line of any kind or any pipe carrying wash water, salt water or other non-potable liquid should pass through potable water tanks. If this is unavoidable, pipes should only pass through potable water tanks in a watertight tunnel that is self-draining. Similarly, it is best that soil waste drains not pass over potable water tanks or wash-water tank manholes. It is also best if toilets and bathroom spaces do not extend over any part of a deck that forms the top of a potable water or wash-water tank.

Every potable water storage tank will need to be provided with a vent located and constructed to prevent the entrance of contaminating substances and vectors. For example, the opening of the vent should be protected by a tight mesh to prevent the entrance of insects. Because of the ship's movement, increased air exchange may take place in potable water tanks. To avoid intrusion of harmful particles, filters that are designed to exclude substances such as dirt and exhaust gases should be used. These filters need to be cleaned or exchanged regularly. Ventilating pipes should not end directly above the water surface, to avoid substances dripping into the water body. A potable water tank vent should not be connected to the vent of any tank holding, or intended for holding, non-potable liquid, as cross-contamination may occur.

It is important that the potable water tank be provided with an overflow or relief valve, located so that the test head of the tank is not exceeded. The overflow must be constructed and protected in the same manner recommended for vents. An overflow may be combined with a vent, but the provisions described for the construction and protection of both vents and overflows must be observed.

The potable water tank should be designed to be completely drained in case there is a need to dump water to remove contamination. The end of the tank suction line should be no closer than 50 mm above the tank bottom, to avoid the intake of sediment or biofilms.

Any means provided for determining the depth of water in potable water tanks should be constructed to prevent the entrance of contaminated substances or liquids. Potable water tanks need to be equipped with facilities to read the filling level of the tank from outside. This construction should not produce areas of stagnating water that could become a source of contamination. Manual sounding should not be performed, as this may lead to unnecessary contamination of the potable water.

All potable water tanks need to be clearly labelled with their capacity and words such as "POTABLE WATER TANK".

The potable water tank will need an inspection cover giving access for cleaning, repair and maintenance. To avoid contamination when opening the cover, the opening should not give direct access to the unprotected water surface. Construction rules should be in line with standardized international regulations. An inspection of the empty tank should be performed periodically (e.g. once per year). If tanks are entered by people, clean protective clothing should be worn. Staff should be equipped with a clean, single-use overall, face mask, disposable rubber gloves and rubber boots that are light in colour, very clean and used only inside potable water tanks. Boots and any tools used in the tank need to be disinfected before entering. No people with any acute illness (e.g. diarrhoea) should be allowed to enter potable water tanks.

Sample cocks should be installed directly on each tank to allow tests to be taken to verify water quality and must point downwards to avoid contamination. Sample cocks should be made of material that allows disinfection and contact with flames for sterilizing. Cold potable water should always be stored at temperatures below 25 °C. More detailed information about technical requirements of potable water tanks can be found in ISO 15748-1.

Potable water tanks and any parts of the potable water distribution system shall be cleaned, disinfected and flushed with potable water:

- before being placed in service; and
- before returning to operation after repair or replacement; or
- after being subjected to any contamination, including entry into a potable water tank.

Potable water tanks shall be inspected, cleaned and disinfected during dry docks and wet docks or every two years, whichever is less.

Disinfection following potential contamination shall be accomplished by increasing free residual halogen to at least 50 mg/l throughout the affected area and maintaining this concentration for 4 hours, or by way of another procedure recognized by WHO.

Potable water pumps

The potable water pump needs the capacity for regular servicing. To prevent contamination, the pump should not be used for any purpose other than pumping potable water. A filter can be installed in the suction line of the pump. Filters need to be maintained according to the manufacturer's instructions (e.g. exchange or regularly backwash). The installation of a standby pump is recommended for emergencies, such as breakdown in the main unit serving the potable water system.

If this secondary pump and piping are filled with water, they must be operated alternating with the primary pump to avoid buildup of microbial contamination in stagnating water. Hand pumps, installed on some ships to serve galleys and pantries for emergency or routine use as a supplement to pressure outlets, need to be constructed and installed to prevent the entrance of contamination. Pumps should ensure continuous operation when required to maintain pressurization—for example, by priming automatically. A direct connection from the pump, with no air gap, should be used when supplying to a potable water tank.

Hydrophore

Hydrophore tanks are used to pressurize the potable water installation and facilitate the transport of the water through the system. In extended potable water installations, permanent running potable water pumps are used instead of hydrophore tanks to establish a continuous positive pressure at all taps.

Hydrophore tanks need to meet the same criteria as other potable water tanks. The tanks should be equipped with maintenance openings for cleaning. They should be of adequate size and located away from any heat sources. Where compressed air is used to produce the air cushion inside the hydrophore tank, a filter, liquid trap or similar device must be installed in the supply line from the compressed air system to protect the water supply. More detailed information can be found in the ISO standards.

Calorifier

Calorifiers are used to produce hot water. In small potable water systems, a so-called decentralized hot-water production system can be used wherever hot water is needed. In more extended installations, however, a central hot-water production unit is typically installed in combination with a hot-water circulation system. Calorifiers should meet the same materials and construction criteria as all other parts of the potable water system. They should be equipped with a maintenance opening and with thermal insulation. To avoid the growth of *Legionella* spp., hot water should leave the calorifier at a temperature of at least 60 °C. A hot-water circulation system should be used, and the returning water should not be colder than 50 °C.

Water distribution system

Ships should have plumbing suitable to protect water safety. Before being supplied, new ships should be inspected for compliance with the design specifications by the relevant competent authority or other authorized independent body. Technical standards such as ISO standards should be considered. A clear and accurate layout of the engineered system on the ship is likely to be needed to support this inspection.

Materials in contact with water need to be safe for the intended purpose. To help ensure this, in new construction and in repairs and replacements on old ships, new pipes, tubing or fittings should be used in the potable water system and in the wash-water system when wash water may be used to supplement potable water after treatment. All materials used should be acceptable to the national health administration of the country of registration. Lead and cadmium materials should not be in contact with water via pipes, fittings and joints and should not be used anywhere in the potable water system, as these can leach into and contaminate the water.

Potable water piping should be clearly identifiable to help prevent cross-connection plumbing errors. To identify potable water piping, a colour code according to international standards (ISO 14726: blue–green–blue) can be used.

Crew must be trained to take hygienic precautions when laying new pipes or repairing existing pipes. It is important in designing the ship to minimize the points where water could collect and become warm (>25 °C) and stagnant. For example, temperature-control valves that prevent scalding must be fitted as close to the point of use as possible to minimize the formation of warm-water pockets. The number of distribution system dead ends should be minimized.

If hot-water piping and cold-water piping are laid side by side, appropriate thermal insulation must be applied to prevent warming or cooling of the respective pipes and the possibility of bacterial growth.

All piping components should be able to resist water temperatures of 90 °C, to facilitate thermal disinfection whenever necessary.

The distribution system should be designed to avoid the bypassing of any important treatment or storage processes.

Fixtures (taps, showerheads)

Fixtures and fittings can harbour contamination, and the design needs to consider how to select suitable attributes to control these risks. To maintain their integrity, an accepted safe practice is to ensure that all fixtures are resistant to the corrosive effects of salt water and saline atmospheres. In addition, fixtures must be easy to clean and designed to function efficiently. To aid cleaning, rounded internal corners are preferred, wherever practicable.

All fixtures should be able to resist water temperatures of at least 70 °C to facilitate thermal disinfection whenever necessary.

Potable water outlets must be labelled "POTABLE WATER". Similarly, non-potable outlets must be labelled "UNFIT FOR DRINKING". To encourage use of the safe potable supply, potable water outlets must be provided in convenient locations, such as near passenger, officer and crew quarters and in the engine and boiler rooms. To support food safety, hot and cold potable water must be supplied under pressure to the galley, pantry and scullery. Steam to be applied directly to food must be made from potable water. Boiler steam is a safe means of heating potable water and food if applied indirectly, through coils, tubes or separate chambers. Hot and cold potable water must be supplied under pressure to the medical care spaces for hand-washing and care purposes. Only potable water must be piped to the freezer for making ice for drinking purposes.

A wash-water system, when installed, can be used to supply slop sinks, laundry facilities, water closets, bibcock connections for deck flushing purposes, heated water for dishwashing and water for other special uses. Wash-water storage tanks shall be constructed and protected so as to prevent the possibility of contamination in a similar way to potable water. Any faucets on the wash-water system must be clearly marked "UNFIT FOR DRINKING".

Washbasins should have hot and cold potable water lines ending in a simple mixing outlet to help control growth of bacteria that would otherwise proliferate in warm-water lines. It is useful to encourage hygienic behaviour by passengers and crew by placing a sign above the basin with instructions to "WASH BASIN BEFORE AND AFTER USE".

Seldom-used taps or showers have a risk of high microbial growth due to water stagnation. This can lead to contamination of the whole distribution system and should be avoided. Therefore, seldom-used fixtures should be regularly flushed for a few minutes to mitigate this risk. A flushing schedule can be a useful tool to ensure that flushing is performed during regular maintenance.

The potable hot-water system, including showerheads, shall be maintained to minimize the growth of pathogenic *Mycobacterium* or *Legionella* bacteria. Showerheads should be cleaned and disinfected every six months. Aerators may harbour very high numbers of pathogenic bacteria such as *Pseudomonas aeruginosa*. Therefore, the aerators should be regularly cleaned and disinfected.

2. Operational limits, monitoring and corrective actions

Disinfection

When treatment, purification or disinfection is necessary, the method selected should be recommended by the competent authority under the IHR 2005 and should be easily operated and maintained by the ship's officers and crew. Disinfection is most efficient when the water has already been treated to remove turbidity and when substances exerting a disinfectant demand or capable of protecting pathogens from disinfection have been removed. However, disinfection does not always eliminate all infectious agents. For example, cross-contamination can easily affect water with a low residual disinfection. Furthermore, parasites such as *Cryptosporidium* produce oocysts that are very resistant to chlorine or chloramine disinfection and need to be removed by filtration or inactivated by an alternative method, such as UV irradiation.

In extended distribution systems, a residual disinfectant should be maintained to limit the growth of microbial hazards that can impart off-flavours to the water and foul lines and fittings. Maintaining residual disinfection (e.g. free chlorine at >0.5 mg/l) will contribute to the control of *Legionella* spp., for instance. In addition, this residual may kill very low levels of some pathogens that may gain entry to the network.

Where chlorine is used as the disinfectant, a satisfactory chlorine residual (typically around 0.5–1 mg/l for free chlorine or 1 mg/l for chloramines as water enters the distribution or storage system) should be maintained.

The disinfectant residual for chlorine (the most common disinfectant) should ideally be no less than 0.2 mg/l and no more than 5 mg/l. For effective primary disinfection, there should be a residual free chlorine concentration of at least 0.5 mg/l after at least 30 minutes' contact time at a pH below 8.0. The chlorine residual should be maintained throughout the distribution system; at the point of delivery, the minimum residual concentration of free chlorine should be 0.2 mg/l.

A pH above 8.0 will decrease the disinfecting effect of chlorine significantly. Test kits to check pH before any disinfection and the level of free and total chlorine during disinfection should be available on board and used as per the manufacturer's specifications.

These normal residuals are not adequate, and should not be relied upon, to disinfect large ingress events. Presence of the residual disinfectant does not mean that water is necessarily safe. Similarly, absence of a residual does not mean that the water is necessarily unsafe if the source is secure and distribution is fully protected.

Process control parameters, such as disinfectant residuals at water disinfection plants and at the farthest tap (e.g. bridge deck), should be monitored at a sufficient frequency to detect deviations in control processes early enough to prevent contaminated water from reaching users, which ideally means continuous automated monitoring.

Absence of a residual where one would normally be found can be a useful indicator of cross-contamination. However, many viral and parasitic pathogens are resistant to low levels of disinfectant, so residual disinfection should not be relied upon to treat contaminated water. Low levels of residual may inactivate bacterial indicators such as *E. coli* and mask contamination that might harbour more resistant pathogens. In such cases, superchlorination treatment is typically applied to destroy the resistant viral and parasitic pathogens. Superchlorination involves various combinations of time and concentration—for instance, dosing chlorine to give a final chlorine residual of around 20 mg/l after 1 hour of contact time.

Whenever the potable water tanks and system or any of their parts have been placed in service, repaired, replaced or contaminated, they must be cleaned, disinfected and flushed before being returned to operation. Where a water distiller is connected to the potable water tank or system, the pipe and appurtenances between the distiller and the potable water tank or system must be disinfected and thoroughly flushed with potable water.

If UV light is intended for disinfection, these devices need to be approved by the national authorities. UV devices need regular maintenance, including cleaning and lamp exchange, according to the manufacturer's instructions. Typically, UV devices should be installed vertically to avoid accumulation of sediments on the lamp. Bypass around UV devices is neither allowed nor useful because of the increased risk of contaminating the whole system. In the case of high turbidity, pre-filters should be used before UV devices to ensure that the unit is operating within the manufacturer's specifications. It should be considered that UV light has no residual effect and that all water needs direct contact with the light.

Chemical parameters

Temperature, pH, hardness and alkalinity are controlled within appropriate ranges for the particular water type to minimize corrosivity and potential leaching of metals. Metals such as lead, nickel, iron, cadmium or copper can be leached from some materials into the water and contribute to adverse taste or, in some cases, health concerns. Excess copper or iron can cause a metallic taste; copper can cause gastrointestinal upset; and excess lead can cause cognitive deficits after long-term high-level exposure in young children. The GDWQ guideline value for copper is 2 mg/l; iron can be detectable by taste at about 0.3 mg/l; and the lead (provisional) guideline value is 0.01 mg/l. In lieu of, or in addition to, monitoring for metals, appropriate management should be achieved through a corrosion control programme.

Disinfectant residuals should be monitored throughout the distribution system.

Physical and aesthetic parameters

Electrical conductivity of the water should be measured whenever water is produced on board. A very low electrical conductivity gives information about a malfunction in the remineralization process.

Turbidity in the potable water on the ship could indicate a gross contamination with biological material or that dirt has entered the system during delivery.

No undesirable tastes, colours or odours should be present in the drinking-water. Aesthetic parameters such as undesirable taste, colour or odour that appear after water treatment may indicate corrosion or cross-connections, contamination by foreign substances during transfer to the ship or inadequate plumbing conditions on board. Complaints about aesthetic parameters (odour, colour or taste) should trigger further investigations into water quality and may indicate the need to monitor turbidity. All these parameters signify the need to determine their cause and to take corrective actions so that water on the ship is both potable and palatable. Furthermore, water that is not aesthetically acceptable will not be consumed, and passengers and crew may instead consume alternative, less safe water.

Cool water is generally more palatable than warm water, and temperature will have an impact on the acceptability of a number of other inorganic constituents that may affect taste. High water temperature enhances the growth of microorganisms and may increase taste, odour, colour and corrosion problems (WHO, 2011).

The occurrence of *Legionella* spp. in high numbers in drinking-water supplies is preventable through implementation of basic water quality management measures, including maintaining piped water temperatures outside the range at which *Legionella* spp. proliferate to high levels (25–50 °C). This can be achieved by setting heaters to ensure that hot water is delivered to all taps at or above 50 °C (which can mean requiring temperatures above 55 °C at the recirculating point and in the return line of hot-water circulation systems) and insulating all pipes and storage tanks to ensure that water is maintained outside the temperature range 25–50 °C. However, maintaining operating temperatures of hot-water systems above 50 °C may result in increased energy requirements and present a scalding risk for young children, the elderly and mentally handicapped persons. In cold-water distribution systems, temperatures should be maintained at less than 25 °C throughout the system to provide effective control. However, this may not be achievable in all systems, particularly those in hot climates. Maintaining disinfectant residuals above 0.2 mg/l throughout the piped distribution system and storage tanks will contribute to the control of *Legionella* spp. in such circumstances. Disinfection devices using UV light can be installed in the distribution system to reduce the risk of contamination by *Legionella* spp. Water flow in the distribution system should also be maintained during periods of reduced activity (Bartram et al., 2007).

Prevention of backflow

When potable water is delivered to non-potable systems and supplied under pressure, the system must be protected against backflow by either backflow preventers or air gaps. If backflow preventers fail, negative pressure can arise, and this can lead to ingress of contaminants into the system. The ship should have a comprehensive programme that provides safe connections to the potable water system through air gaps or appropriate backflow-prevention devices at high-hazard locations.

To prevent contamination, it is advisable to ensure that the potable water system is not connected to any non-potable water system. To achieve this, overflows, vents and drains from tanks, and drains from the distribution system must not be connected directly to sewage drains. When drain lines are extended towards the bottom of the ship, they must terminate a suitable distance above the inner-bottom plating or above the highest point of the bilge in the absence of such plating, unless backflow is impossible. Air gaps and receiving funnels must be installed in these lines when they discharge to a closed tank of a non-potable water, to a deck drain or to a sanitary drain. Potable water piping must not pass under or through sewage tanks, or pipes or tanks holding non-potable liquids. The distribution lines, including suction lines of the potable water pump, should not be cross-connected with the piping or storage tanks of any non-potable water system. Potable water lines must be located so that they will not be submerged in bilge water or pass through tanks storing non-potable liquids.

Examples of areas where backflow prevention may be used are:

- potable water supply lines to swimming pools, whirlpools, hot tubs, bathtubs, showers and similar facilities;
- photographic laboratory developing machines;
- beauty and barber shop spray-rinse hoses;
- garbage grinders;
- hospital and laundry equipment;
- air-conditioning expansion tanks;
- boiler-feed water tanks;
- fire systems;
- toilets;
- freshwater or saltwater ballast systems;
- bilge water or other wastewater locations;
- international shore connections;
- any other connection between the potable and non-potable water systems.

Each backflow preventer must be scheduled for inspection and service in accordance with the manufacturer's instructions and as necessary to prevent the device's failure. To facilitate this, backflow preventers should be located in easily accessible areas. A standard backflow preventer or other device to prevent the flow of water from ship to shore must be installed on every ship. Drainage to prevent freezing may need to be provided. The ship's crew needs to undertake, or commission, regular checks and tests on the adequacy of backflow preventers, possible cross-connection points, leaks, defective pipes, pressure and disinfectant residuals. This should be included in a routine, comprehensive sanitary inspection programme.

Individual air gaps must be placed in drain lines from certain types of fixtures, such as refrigeration units and all hospital, food preparation and food-servicing equipment, when such drainage is to a system that receives sewage or hospital wastes, unless, for example, drains are independent of each other and of all other drainage systems.

The sanitary or overboard water system, including all pumps, piping and fixtures, should be completely independent of the potable water and wash-water systems. All faucets and outlets on the sanitary system should be clearly labelled "UNFIT FOR DRINKING". Any bidets installed should be of the jet type, and any potable or wash-water line serving them should be equipped with a backflow preventer.

To control cross-contamination, saltwater service to bathtubs and showers must be independent, with no cross-connections to either the potable water or wash-water systems.

When a ship is without power to operate its pumps, it may connect its firefighting system to the shore potable water system. If the connection remains after the ship's power system is restored, the non-potable water from the ship's firefighting system may accidentally be pumped back into the shore potable water system. Measures should be put in place to ensure that this does not occur.

Verification monitoring

Regular water quality monitoring must be performed to demonstrate that source water being supplied to the port and potable water on board are not contaminated with fresh faecal material or other microbial and chemical hazards. Regular monitoring of each parameter is necessary to ensure that safe water quality is maintained, as each step in the water transfer chain provides an opportunity for contamination. Monitoring needs to be specific in terms of what, how, when and who. The focus for the control of process operations should be on simple measurements that must be done online and in the field. In most cases, routine monitoring will be based on simple surrogate observations or tests, such as turbidity or structural integrity, rather than complex microbial or chemical tests. Infrastructure should be monitored (e.g. checks for filter cracks and pipe leaks, defective backflow preventers or cross-connections). Filters need to be exchanged or backwashed according to the manufacturer's instructions. Seldom-used taps and showers should be flushed regularly to avoid microbial growth due to stagnating water, with both actions described in the WSP. Disinfection must be monitored online by measurements of residual disinfectant, turbidity, pH and temperature; a direct feedback and control system must be included. As such tests can be carried out rapidly, they are often preferred to microbiological testing. It is essential that all monitoring equipment be calibrated for accuracy and checked against independent readings. Records of readings must be documented. Periodic sanitary surveys of the storage and distribution system are an important part of any WSP. These are inexpensive to carry out and can complement routine water quality measurements.

Monitoring actions need to provide information in sufficient time that corrective action can be taken to ensure that process controls will prevent contaminated water from reaching passengers and crew.

Aesthetic parameters such as odour, colour or taste are typically "measured" through consumer complaints, although the crew may also wish to do an independent periodic check. This is a subjective parameter, as individuals have different sensitivities.

Some countries may request additional monitoring for parameters over and above those suggested by the GDWQ within their jurisdiction, for operational or regulatory reasons. Ports and ship operators should verify with their local authority whether additional monitoring is required. This should be included in the WSP.

Investigative and corrective action

In the event of contamination of water on the ship, the ship's operator or master should notify persons on board who may be affected to take immediate mitigation measures or arrange for an alternative water supply. Appropriate action may include additional treatment, or flushing and disinfection of transfer equipment or ship water tanks.

Specific corrective actions must be developed for each control measure in the WSP to deal with deviations when they occur. The actions must ensure that the control point has been brought under control. They may include repair of defective filters, repair or replacement of pipes or tanks or breaking of cross-connections.

The ability to change temporarily to alternative water sources is one of the most useful corrective actions available but is not always possible. Backup disinfection plans may be necessary.

Investigative action and response could be as basic as reviewing records or could include more comprehensive corrective action. Corrective action should involve remedying any mechanical, operational or procedural defect in the water supply system that has led to critical limits or guideline values being exceeded. In the case of mechanical defects, remedies should include maintenance, upgrading or refurbishment of facilities. In the case of operational defects, actions should include changes to supplies and equipment. In the case of procedural defects, such as improper practices, standard operating procedures and training programmes should be evaluated and changed, with personnel retrained. Any such changes should be incorporated into the WSP.

The competent authority under the IHR 2005 should be informed whenever required by the national regulations of the port State and in all cases of illnesses and/or complex problems on board. Reporting of illnesses and sanitary conditions that may pose a public health risk (e.g. water system in poor condition) is an international obligation under the IHR 2005.

Oversight should be provided to ensure that corrective actions are implemented in accordance with written procedures and quickly enough to minimize exposure of the travelling public and crew members. Oversight could be performed by the responsible party for that segment of the supply chain or by an independent party, such as a regulatory authority.

Emergency or contingency actions may need to be taken, such as provision of water from alternative sources. During periods when corrective action is being taken, increased monitoring is required.

3. Management and communication

Verification monitoring

Verification monitoring of potable water on the ship is carried out at locations selected to ensure that persons on board are provided with safe water. Verification steps should be adequate to provide assurance that water quality has been maintained at, or restored to, safe levels. It is important to separate verification monitoring from less sophisticated measures such as simple on-site tests and more complex procedures such as sampling for microbiological and chemical laboratory analysis. While simple on-site tests (e.g. regular verification and operational monitoring of pH and chlorination) can be performed by appropriately trained and competent ship staff, sampling for complex chemical and/or microbiological analysis should always be performed by well-trained professional persons who are authorized by a certified laboratory. Only special sampling containers (e.g. sterile glass bottles that contain sodium thiosulfate for microbiological samples or special polyethylene bottles for chemical samples) should be used. Usually samples are taken in one port, and the ship will leave port while the results are still pending. Often the results need to be interpreted by the next port, and therefore it is desirable to follow a defined sampling scheme and sampling procedures (e.g. according to ISO 19458) to provide internationally comparable results.

A standard sampling scheme should be developed for each ship, depending on the size and complexity of the potable water system. At a minimum, it is diligent to take a sample directly from the tank (sampling taps are necessary) and one sample at the farthest point of the distribution system (e.g. tap at the bridge deck). The tank sample gives information about the quality of the water supply on board, while the bridge sample gives information about the quality of the water for the consumer. If both samples have been taken at the same time, they can be compared to provide information about the influence of the distribution system. This is an easy and affordable way to obtain a quick overview of the system's status.

Sampling guidelines for physicochemical and microbiological analysis can be found in Volume 3 of the 2nd edition of the GDWQ, *Surveillance and control of community supplies* (WHO, 1997), and in ISO 19458:2006—Water quality—Sampling for microbiological analysis.

Detailed information about useful sampling schemes, sampling procedures, standard parameters and action triggers is given in section 2.2.4.

Laboratories engaged for potable water analysis should refer to international quality standards (e.g. ISO/IEC 17025).

It is recommended that *E. coli* or thermotolerant (faecal) coliforms be monitored at representative taps (e.g. drinking fountains). Monitoring should take place at each major servicing, in addition to regular *E. coli* spot checks while in service.

HPC can be used as an indicator of general water quality within the distribution system. An increase in HPC indicates post-treatment contamination, regrowth within the water conveyed by the distribution system or the presence of deposits and biofilms in the system. A sudden increase in HPC above historical baseline values should trigger actions to investigate and, if necessary, remediate the situation.

Testing for *Legionella* bacteria serves as a form of verification that the controls are working. It should be undertaken periodically, such as monthly, quarterly or annually, depending on the type of ship environment and the climate of the shipping passage. This testing should not replace or pre-empt the emphasis on control strategies. Furthermore, the tests are relatively specialized and need to be undertaken by properly equipped laboratories with experienced staff. Verification sampling should focus on system extremities and high-risk sites.

Pseudomonas aeruginosa can cause a range of infections but rarely causes serious illness in healthy individuals without some predisposing factor. It predominantly colonizes damaged sites such as burns and surgical wounds, the respiratory tracts of people with underlying disease and physically damaged eyes. From these sites, it may invade the body, causing destructive lesions or septicaemia and meningitis. *Pseudomonas aeruginosa* can multiply in water environments and also on the surface of suitable organic materials in contact with water. *Pseudomonas* can be found frequently in aerators and showerheads. The presence of high numbers of *P. aeruginosa* in potable water can be associated with complaints about taste, odour and turbidity. If there is any evidence of stagnating water or inappropriate maintenance of taps and showerheads (especially in medical areas), a test for occurrence of *P. aeruginosa* should be completed.

The principal concern for toxic chemicals in potable water on board is most likely metals, such as lead, nickel, iron, cadmium or copper, or other chemicals leached from the distribution system into the water that can contribute to adverse taste or, in some cases, health concerns. For ships that produce their own water from seawater, other chemicals may be of concern, such as boron and bromide. The choice of chemicals to be monitored depends on the situation. All samples need to meet GDWQ or national standards (whichever are stricter) for chemicals with potentially significant effects associated with chronic exposures.

In certain situations, the frequency of monitoring should be increased for a period necessary to determine appropriate corrective action and/or provide assurance that measured parameters have been maintained at, or returned to, safe levels. Examples of situations warranting increased monitoring are positive *E. coli* or thermotolerant (faecal) coliform results, excessively humid conditions, natural disasters affecting source water quality, significant increase in HPC and maintenance activities that have the potential to affect water quality.

Record keeping

Documentation of monitoring should be kept for assurance and analysis in the event of an incident. Documentation should be showed to the competent authority under the IHR 2005 whenever requested.

Documentation of inspection, maintenance, cleaning, disinfection (to include concentration and contact time of disinfectant) and flushing shall be maintained for 12 months and shall be available.

Training

Crew should be suitably trained by experienced professionals in all aspects of their operation and maintenance of the water supply system. Examples of specific training areas are aspects of bunkering procedures, onboard water production, temperature and stagnation, maintenance of the water system and all treatment components.

2.2.4 Guideline 2.4: Independent surveillance

Guideline 2.4—Independent surveillance of potable water safety is performed by a competent authority under the IHR 2005.

Indicators for Guideline 2.4

1. Audit/inspection procedures are put in place by a competent authority under the IHR 2005.
2. Documentation and implementation of a WSP are reviewed, and feedback is provided.
3. An independent competent authority under the IHR 2005 responds to reports of incidents with the potential to adversely affect public health.

Guidance notes for Guideline 2.4

One limitation with water quality monitoring is that, by the time contamination is detected, it is likely that some of the contaminated water has been consumed. Therefore, surveillance should extend to auditing, whereby the processes in place to protect water quality are checked on board ship and at port by an appropriately experienced auditor.

Ship water quality surveillance is an ongoing investigative activity that is undertaken to identify and evaluate potential health risks associated with the use and consumption of potable water on board. Surveillance protects public health by promoting the improvement of quality, quantity, accessibility and continuity of potable water supplies. This guideline addresses surveillance of these factors only and does not address surveillance relating to monitoring of, or response to, outbreaks or other disease events (i.e. public health surveillance).

Levels of surveillance of drinking-water quality differ widely. Surveillance should be developed and expanded progressively, by adapting the level to the local situation and economic resources, with gradual implementation, consolidation and development of the programme to the level ultimately desired. When accepting a WSP, the competent authority under the IHR 2005 in a given jurisdiction may take responsibility for surveillance of the programme, which may include performing random water sampling and auditing the WSP programme.

Although this guideline addresses surveillance by oversight authorities, many concepts discussed could be employed by the water supplier to ensure that the WSP is being implemented effectively.

1. Establishment of procedures

In most cases, surveillance consists primarily of sanitary inspections, based on the WSP, of ports, watering facilities or ships. Sanitary inspection is a tool for determining the state of the water supply infrastructure and identification of actual or potential faults and should be carried out regularly.

A State health inspector should have the authority to conduct independent inspections and verify the reliability of the supplier's information. This does not normally need to be as frequent as the continuous control performed by ports and ship operators.

Surveillance should be accomplished by authorized and trained officers from public health authorities. Alternatively, the services of qualified independent auditors may be used if they have been authorized by the relevant competent health authority.

Specifications for qualifications of the inspectors should be established, and inspectors should undergo adequate training, including periodic updates and recertification. Independent auditors and inspectors should meet the same requirements as those from the public health authorities.

2. Review of documentation and plan implementation

WSPs should be provided by the port authority and the ship operators, and all documentation pertaining to the WSPs should be reviewed. The independent review of the WSPs should include a systematic approach, based on the components of the WSPs, by external auditing of the documentation, implementation and monitoring of critical control points.

Components of the independent review include inspection of crew personal hygiene through the demonstration of crew members following procedures, inspections of equipment and environmental conditions to ensure that dedicated equipment is used and stored under sanitary conditions, recording these inspections, and water sampling through on-site or laboratory tests. Periodic microbiological surveillance of the entire water supply system from the source to representative taps on board should be a key priority because of the acute risk to health posed by pathogens in drinking-water. Verification of compliance with water standards should start at the source and extend throughout the water distribution system. Each water source, transfer point or critical point in the distribution system and end-point should be monitored. If this is not possible, at a minimum, end-points and tanks should be monitored, but it should be possible to trace back when an unsatisfactory result is found.

Inspection of procedures or control systems should be adequate to provide assurance that responsible parties in the water supply chain are able to implement timely corrective measures. Supporting programmes should be reviewed to ensure that management procedures and training are adequate to maintain a safe supply of water.

Communication procedures by and to the water supplier, port authority, delivery points, ship operator and the public should also be reviewed. A notification system should be established that integrates all parties within the water supply and transfer chain.

3. Response to incidents

Response to incidents may include written reports from the responsible party or independent inspectors or written or verbal reports from affected individuals or their representatives. The competent authority under the IHR 2005 should investigate reports of incidents by interviewing reporters, responsible parties and other affected individuals and independently verifying water quality and relevant process parameters (maintenance checklists, training records, etc.) through on-site inspections and other means. The competent authority under the IHR 2005 should coordinate with and advise responsible parties on appropriate corrective actions (modifications to water safety, management, training and maintenance plans, notification of potentially affected individuals, etc.) and ensure that remedial action plans are effective and implemented.

Sampling scheme

Sampling must be done by professionally trained personnel only. Sampling procedures for microbiological testing of potable water are described in ISO 19458. Laboratories should analyse the water according to internationally accepted technical standards, such as ISO/IEC 17025. It is important that sampling methods and analytical procedures are comparable from laboratory to laboratory and from State to State. Examples of parameters frequently tested in potable water and typical values are given in Table 2-2.

Table 2-2 Examples of parameters frequently tested in potable water and typical values

Parameter	Typical value	Unit	Comments
pH[a]	6.5–9.5	–	Ideal pH depends on the materials used. A pH above 8.0 does not allow effective water disinfection with chlorine and gives evidence that self-produced water may not be remineralized adequately. Further assessment of potable water quality should be performed.
Temperature, cold water[b]	5–25	°C	Ideally below 20 °C to avoid growth of *Legionella* spp. If above 25 °C, a high risk of *Legionella* spp. contamination exists. Violation should trigger testing for contamination with *Legionella* spp.
Temperature, hot water[b]	50–90	°C	To prevent growth of *Legionella* spp., temperatures above 55 °C should be maintained in hot-water storages and whole piping system.[a] Violation should trigger testing for contamination with *Legionella* spp.
Conductivity	–	µS/cm	Indirect measure of total dissolved solids Typical values (approximately): Untreated distillate: 50 µS/cm Water from shore sources: 500 µS/cm Seawater: 50 000 µS/cm Too low conductivity should trigger evaluation of corrosive processes in the piping and existence of heavy metals due to corrosion.
Hardness[a] (calcium carbonate)	>100	mg/l	Hardness below 60 mg/l poses high risk of copper corrosion. Too low hardness should trigger evaluation of corrosive processes in the piping and existence of heavy metals due to corrosion.
Turbidity[a]	1	NTU	Turbidity should be below 1 NTU for effective disinfection.
Escherichia coli	0	cfu/100 ml	ISO 9308-1/2:1990

Table 2-2 Examples of parameters frequently tested in potable water and typical values *continued*

Parameter	Typical value	Unit	Comments
HPC (at 20 °C)	No abnormal deviations	cfu/100 ml	–
HPC (at 37 °C)	No abnormal deviations	cfu/100 ml	–
Legionella spp.	<100	cfu/100 ml	Temperature should be above 55 °C in hot water and below 25 °C in cold water to avoid excessive growth of *Legionella* spp.
Lead[a]	10	µg/l	–
Copper[a]	2000	µg/l	Copper has been shown to cause acute gastrointestinal discomfort and nausea at concentrations above about 3 mg/l.
Cadmium[a]	3	µg/l	–
Iron[a]	200	µg/l	–
Nickel[a]	70	µg/l	The concentration of nickel in drinking-water is normally less than 20 µg/l.
Zinc[a]	3000	µg/l	–
Chlorine, free[a]	<5	mg/l	For effective disinfection, there should be a residual concentration of free chlorine of at least 0.5 mg/l after at least 30 minutes' contact time at pH below 8.
Chlorine dioxide[b]	0.05	mg/l	–
Colour	<15	TCU	No visible colour

–, not available; cfu, colony-forming units; HPC, heterotrophic plate count; NTU, nephelometric turbidity units; TCU, true colour units.

[a] WHO (2011).

[b] ISO 15748-1:2002—Ships and marine technology—Potable water supply on ships and marine structures—Part 1: Planning and design.

Before a standard sampling scheme can be defined, it is necessary to consider that there are two reasons for sampling:

- standard surveillance to perform verification of good management
- more detailed inspection in case of suspected problems.

In case of suspected problems, either a broad assessment or a focused search in the system can be completed. The sampling should be performed after an inspection of the whole system. WHO's *Recommended procedures for inspection of ships and issuance of ship sanitation certificates* (WHO, 2010) provide more detailed information for a system assessment on board. When monitoring, a standard sampling scheme can be very useful to provide reliable and comparable information.

The explanations below give information about how to select a sampling point, action triggers to decide which parameters should be examined and procedures for taking samples.

All procedures should be discussed in advance with the laboratory that will analyse the samples to avoid any misunderstandings.

If the water has been produced on board or water has been bunkered from ashore, the water quality in the ship's tank gives information about the source water quality. Sampling should be performed directly from a defined and labelled sampling tap installed at the tank, referring to a suitable procedure such as that described in ISO 19458 purpose "A": "Disinfect or sterilize the sampling tap with a gas burner or with suitable disinfection liquid (e.g. Ethanol 70%), let water flow out until the temperature is constant (or at least 10 litres if directly taken from the tank) and fill the sterile sampling bottle".

Where water is used for human consumption on board ship, it has to be potable. If information is needed about the influence of the distribution system, the farthest tap should be examined to inform the assessor of the highest potential risk. This tap typically can be found at the bridge deck. Here an additional sample should be taken, referring to a suitable procedure such as ISO 19458 purpose "B": "Remove aerator, clean the tap, disinfect or sterilize the tap by using disinfection liquid or gas burner, let some water flow out (approximately 2–3 Litres) and fill the sterile sampling bottle".

Whenever the water temperature is between 25 °C and 50 °C, a high risk of contamination by *Legionella* spp. exists. The main risk is that contaminated aerosols can be inhaled (e.g. in the shower). Therefore, at least one shower should be examined within a monitoring programme. It is useful to take a cold-water and hot-water sample from the same shower to avoid unnecessary follow-up sampling. Sampling for *Legionella* spp. analysis is not defined in ISO 19458 but could be performed as follows: Choose a sampling point (e.g. showerhead), do not remove the showerhead and hose, do not disinfect the showerhead or hose, open the cold-water tap, let 2–3 litres flow out, take the sample, measure the temperature, let the cold water flow for 5 minutes and measure the temperature again, then close the cold-water tap. Open the hot-water tap, let 2–3 litres flow out, take the sample, measure the temperature, let the hot water flow for 5 minutes and measure the temperature again, then close the hot-water tap. Additionally to the sampling at one shower, a sample at the flow line and at the return line close to the calorifier can be useful to get information on whether the whole system or just the single shower is contaminated.

When evidence is found of stagnating water or otherwise poorly maintained fixtures in medical areas, testing for *Pseudomonas aeruginosa* can be useful. In this case, sampling should refer to a suitable procedure such as ISO 19458 purpose "C": "Choose a sampling point, do not remove aerators or showerheads, do not disinfect or sterilize the fixture or showerhead, open the tap and take the sample immediately". The same sampling procedure should be applied at suspect taps if there is any outbreak on board that may be associated with a waterborne organism.

When there is any evidence of malfunction in water rehardening procedures (e.g. missing pre-acidification, high pH, low conductivity, low hardness, colour changes in water or at surfaces that are in contact with water), a chemical analysis of dissolved metals should be arranged from one tap. Two different methods can be applied:

Method A: Take one sample directly from the tap without any other measures in advance. Usually a polyethylene bottle with a volume of 1 litre would be used. This method requires just one sample but will not provide further information on the contamination source. The disadvantage of this method is that there is no information about the stagnation time of the water in the piping before the sample has been taken.

Method B: Advise the officer in charge on board to begin 4 hours before sampling with the following procedure: Flush the chosen sampling tap (e.g. bridge deck) thoroughly for at least 15–20 minutes, and close and secure the tap against accidental use until the next sample is required (in 4 hours).

For sampling, three polyethylene bottles with a volume of 1 litre should be used.

Bottle 1: Open the tap and fill the bottle immediately.

Bottle 2: Let 2–3 litres of water flow through, and fill the second bottle.

Bottle 3: Let the water flow for at least 15–20 minutes, and fill the third bottle.

The analysis of bottle 1 will give information about influence of the fixture; bottle 2 represents the influence of the piping; and bottle 3 provides information about the water source.

If tank coatings or other materials that are in contact with the potable water appear to render the water unfit for human consumption (e.g. chemical odour), a specialized chemical analysis should be performed.

Whenever water samples are taken on board or ashore, some on-site parameters should be measured, as these can change while samples are transported to the laboratory. These parameters are pH, level of free chlorine, level of total chlorine, conductivity, temperature and turbidity. These values should always be documented, together with detailed information about how and where the samples have been taken.

To obtain reliable and comparable information about the sanitary status of the potable water installation, it is recommended that samples be taken at the same places (e.g. always at the tank and from the bridge deck).

To establish communication between different ports in international travel, it is recommended that the water quality analysis reports be issued in English. The sampling points should be clearly indicated, and all analysis results should be clearly documented. It should be considered that some port States do not accept potable water analysis reports when they do not make clear that the laboratory was working according to a suitable procedure, such as ISO/IEC 17025.

3 Food

3.1 Background

This chapter focuses on foodborne disease, including disease associated with bottled water and ice. The previous chapter (chapter 2) considered disease associated with potable water supplied on board.

3.1.1 Food supply and transfer chain

Foodborne outbreaks have been associated with sourcing unsafe food. Therefore, the first preventive strategy should be to source safe food. Even if the sourced food is safe, measures need to be put in place to ensure that it remains safe during the transfer, storage, preparation and serving activities that follow. An understanding of the ship food supply and transfer chain will help to illustrate the points at which the food can become contaminated en route to the point of consumption.

Generally, the ship food supply and transfer chain consists of five major components that provide multiple opportunities for the introduction, or proliferation, of contaminants in food:

- the source of food coming into the port;
- transfer of food to storage points on board ship;
- storage and general distribution of food on board ship;
- preparation and serving of food, including cooking and mixing by food handlers;
- handling and storage of food for personal consumption by passengers or crew, including taking food away and storing it in private areas for subsequent consumption.

3.1.2 Health risks associated with food on ships

Significant levels of foodborne disease transmission on ships have been reported. The Rooney et al. (2004) review of more than 100 outbreaks associated with ships found that two fifths of the outbreaks reported were foodborne outbreaks. As more than one third of the reviewed outbreaks could not be associated with any specific exposure route, the true contribution from foodborne transmission to the total may be significantly higher. The Rooney et al. (2004) review provided important information on examples, and possible causes, of foodborne disease, and these examples are cited throughout this chapter.

Importantly, the majority of reported foodborne disease outbreaks were caused by pathogenic bacteria such as *Salmonella* spp., *Shigella* spp. and *Vibrio* spp. The symptoms of bacterial infections can be more severe and prolonged than are typically observed with more common viral diseases or *Cryptosporidium* infection. This implies an enhanced morbidity burden due to foodborne disease, which further emphasizes the significance of this exposure route.

Foodborne disease is often referred to generally as "food poisoning", which has, in turn, been defined by WHO as "any disease of an infectious or toxic nature caused by or thought to be caused by the consumption of food". This definition includes all illness, regardless of the presenting symptoms and signs, thought to have been caused by food. The definition includes acute illnesses characterized by diarrhoea and/or vomiting and illnesses presenting with manifestations not related to the gastrointestinal tract, such as scrombotoxin poisoning, paralytic shellfish poisoning, botulism and listeriosis. In addition, the definition includes illness caused by toxic chemicals but excludes illness due to known allergies and food intolerances. Note that "foodborne" refers to the probable source of the infection, not the nature of the signs and symptoms. Many of the signs and symptoms of the diseases that can be foodborne can also be acquired by other routes, such as person-to-person and waterborne transmission.

Foodborne biological hazardous agents include bacteria, viruses, fungi and parasites. These organisms are commonly associated with humans, with raw products entering the food preparation site and with the occurrence of pests. Many of these microorganisms occur naturally in the environment where food is grown. Therefore, some contamination by these pathogens can be expected in raw food.

A range of helminthic and protozoan parasites can contaminate food. Many are zoonotic (capable of infecting many species of animals and humans), so meat and poultry can become directly contaminated at source. Some diseases are transmitted by the faecal–oral route, whereas others are transmitted via consumption of contaminated flesh. Parasitic infections are commonly associated with undercooked meat products or contaminated ready-to-eat food. Some parasites in products that are intended to be eaten raw, marinated or partially cooked can be killed by effective freezing techniques (the precise conditions that are appropriate will depend on the nature of both the food and the parasites).

Chemical contaminants in food may be inadvertently added during the growing phase, be naturally occurring or be added accidentally during processing—for example, by the misuse of cleaning chemicals or pesticides. Examples of naturally occurring chemicals are mycotoxins (e.g. aflatoxin), scombrotoxin (histamine), ciguatoxin, mushroom toxins and shellfish toxins.

Some of the causal hazards associated with foodborne disease outbreaks associated with ships are listed in Table 3-1 (Rooney et al., 2004). Note that in some foodborne outbreaks, the causative agent may not have been identified.

Table 3-1 Agents associated with foodborne disease outbreaks within ships, 1 January 1970 – 30 June 2003

Pathogen/toxin	Number of outbreaks	Number of passengers and crew members affected
Enterotoxigenic *Escherichia coli*	8	2670
Invasive *Escherichia coli*	1	153
Norovirus	4	866
Vibrio spp.	6	1259
Salmonella spp. (non-typhi)	15	1849
Shigella spp.	8	2076
Staphylococcus aureus	2	380
Clostridium perfringens	1	18
Cyclospora spp.	1	220
Trichinella spiralis	1	13
Unknown agent	3	360

Source: Rooney et al. (2004).

Factors contributing to foodborne outbreaks on board ship have included:

- contaminated raw ingredients
- inadequate temperature control
- inadequate heat treatment
- infected food handlers
- use of seawater in the galley.

Bacteria and fungi present significant risks for two reasons:

- Both raw and cooked food can provide a fertile medium and support rapid growth of these organisms. Food can become recontaminated after it has cooled, such that cooked food is not necessarily safe.
- There are toxins of fungal and bacterial origin that are relatively heat stable and can remain at hazardous levels even after cooking.

Therefore, the contamination levels in raw food should be minimized even when cooking occurs.

Unlike bacteria and fungi, human pathogenic viruses are unable to reproduce outside a living cell. In general, they cannot replicate in food and can only be carried by it. Furthermore, most foodborne viruses affecting humans are limited to human hosts. This makes contamination by the unclean hands of infected food handlers or from human faecal contamination the prime risk factors.

The presence of non-potable water on ships can also present additional risks for food contamination. Only potable water should be supplied to the galley, and food should not be held at ambient temperature for extended periods.

Outbreaks have been associated with presymptomatic, symptomatic and post-symptomatic food handlers, and viral shedding can occur from asymptomatic infected individuals. Infected food handlers should be encouraged to report symptoms and be excluded from work until at least 48 hours after symptoms have ceased. Exposed food that will not be cooked, such as fruit, should be discarded if it may have become contaminated.

The pressure on space and facilities on board ship can lead to a lack of adequate facilities and equipment, and this can be a contributing factor in causing disease. For example, in an outbreak of multiple antibiotic-resistant *Shigella flexneri* 4a, the spread of infection by a food handler may have been facilitated by limited availability of toilet facilities for the galley crew (Lew et al., 1991). Conveniently located hand-washing and toilet facilities are a prerequisite for hygienic handling of food.

3.1.3 International Health Regulations (2005)

The IHR 2005 contain provisions for the State Party to designate ports to develop core capacities, such as the capacity to ensure a safe environment for travellers using port facilities, including potable water and eating establishments (Annex 1B1(d) of the IHR 2005).

In accordance with Articles 22(b), 22(e) and 24(c) of the IHR 2005, Member States are required to take all practicable measures to ensure that international conveyance operators keep their conveyances free from sources of contamination and infection, and competent authorities are responsible for ensuring that the facilities at international ports are in sanitary condition and for supervising the removal and safe disposal of any contaminated water and food from a conveyance.

However, it is the responsibility of each ship operator to apply all practicable measures to ensure that no sources of infection and contamination are present on board, including in the water system or food supplies. For this purpose, it is important that these standards are upheld on board ships and at ports, in terms of the safety of the food served, from the source of supply ashore to distribution on board ship.

3.1.4 Overview of food safety plans, and hazard analysis and critical control points

The Codex Alimentarius Commission implements the Joint Food and Agriculture Organization of the United Nations (FAO)/WHO Food Standards Programme, the purpose of which is to protect the health of consumers and to ensure fair practices in the food trade. The Codex Alimentarius is a collection of internationally adopted food standards presented in a uniform manner. It also includes advisory provisions in the form of codes of practice, guidelines and other recommended measures to assist in achieving its purposes (FAO/WHO, 1995, 1997a, 1997b, 1999, 2003). Codex Alimentarius guidance provides important information on basic food safety, which will be referred to throughout this chapter.

The ILO has developed labour standards that include consideration of food and catering requirements and competencies for merchant ships.

Food safety plans (FSPs) are required to manage the process of providing safe food. Typically, the FSP is based around hazard analysis and critical control point (HACCP) methodology, which is described in detail by FAO/WHO (2003), ISO (ISO 22000:2005—Food safety management systems—Requirements for any organization in the food chain) and the National Advisory Committee on Microbiological Criteria for Foods (1997). The base reference in this document for food safety management is HACCP. There may be other acceptable food safety management programmes that involve partial application of the full HACCP system.

A modern FSP would generally be based around HACCP principles and the prerequisite supporting programmes. The FSP is intended to provide a systematic approach to identifying specific hazards and measures for their control to ensure the safety of food. The FSP should be used as a tool to assess hazards and establish control systems that focus on prevention rather than relying mainly on end-product testing. The FSP should be capable of accommodating change, such as changes to the ship menus, layout and equipment; advances in equipment design; changes in processing procedures; or technological developments. FSP implementation should be guided by scientific evidence of risks to human health. As well as enhancing food safety, implementation of an FSP can provide other significant benefits, including a framework to support inspection and certification by regulatory authorities and registrars. The successful implementation of an FSP requires the full commitment and involvement of both management and the workforce.

The prerequisite or supporting programmes that form part of an FSP typically include:

- good design
- quality construction
- hygienic work practices
- training of chefs and food handlers
- quality assurance of raw material ingredients
- operation in accordance with any appropriate food safety legislation.

The core HACCP steps and principles will be briefly described as they relate to ships. It is important when applying HACCP to be flexible, where appropriate, given the context of the application and taking into account the nature and size of the operation.

Preliminary steps

- Step 1. Assemble the HACCP team. The ship operator should ensure that the appropriate knowledge and expertise are available for the development of an effective HACCP plan. The scope of the HACCP plan should be identified.
- Step 2. Describe the products. Full description should be given, including storage conditions.
- Step 3. Identify the intended use of the plan. Vulnerable groups of the population (e.g. the elderly or pregnant women) may have to be considered, as may allergic groups.
- Step 4. Construct flow diagrams. A flow diagram should cover all steps in any given operation.
- Step 5. Conduct on-site confirmation of flow diagrams. The HACCP team should confirm the process operation against the flow diagram and make amendments where necessary.

HACCP principles

- Principle 1: Hazard analysis. The team should list all potential hazards associated with each step, conduct a hazard analysis and consider any measures to control identified hazards. Hazard identification includes defining which hazards are of such a nature that their elimination or reduction to acceptable levels is essential for the preparation of safe food. The HACCP team must then consider whether control measures, if any exist, can be applied to each hazard. More than one control measure may be required to control a specific hazard, and more than one hazard may be controlled by a specified control measure. In conducting the hazard analysis, wherever possible, the following should be included:
  - the likely occurrence of hazards and severity of their health effects;
  - the qualitative and/or quantitative evaluation of the presence of hazards;
  - survival or multiplication of microorganisms of concern;
  - production or persistence in foods of toxins, chemicals or physical agents;
  - conditions leading to the above.
- Principle 2: Determine critical control points (CCPs). CCPs are the stages in the preparation and cooking of food that must be controlled to ensure the safety of the food. There may be more than one CCP at which control is applied to address the same hazard. The determination of a CCP in the HACCP system can be facilitated by the application of a decision-tree, which indicates a logical reasoning approach.
- Principle 3: Establish critical limits for each CCP. Critical limits must be specified and technically validated for each CCP. Criteria often used include temperature, time and available chlorine.
- Principle 4: Establish a monitoring system for each CCP. Monitoring is the scheduled measurement or observation of a CCP relative to its critical limits. The monitoring procedures must be able to detect loss of control at the CCP. Further, monitoring should ideally provide this information in time to make adjustments to ensure control of the process to prevent violation of the critical limits. Where possible, process adjustments should be made when monitoring results indicate a trend towards loss of control at a CCP. If monitoring is not continuous, the amount or frequency of monitoring must be sufficient to guarantee that the CCP is under control.

- Principle 5: Establish corrective actions. Corrective actions must be developed for each CCP in the HACCP system to deal with deviations when they occur. The actions must ensure that the CCP has been brought under control.
- Principle 6: Establish verification procedures. Verification and auditing methods, including random sampling and analysis, can be used to determine if the HACCP system is working correctly. The frequency of verification should be sufficient to confirm that the HACCP system is working effectively.
- Principle 7: Establish documentation and record keeping. Efficient and accurate record keeping is essential to the application of a HACCP system. Documentation and record keeping should be appropriate to the nature and size of the ship.

Training programmes should be routinely reviewed and updated where necessary. Systems should be in place to ensure that food handlers remain aware of all procedures to maintain the safety and suitability of food.

3.2 Guidelines

This section provides targeted information and guidance, identifying responsibilities and providing examples of practices that can control risks. Thirteen specific *guidelines* (situations to aim for and maintain) are presented, each of which is accompanied by a set of *indicators* (measures for whether the guidelines are met) and *guidance notes* (advice on applying the guidelines and indicators in practice, highlighting the most important aspects that need to be considered when setting priorities for action).

The guiding principle for this section is ensuring that food is safe for intended use at the point of consumption.

Guidelines 3.2–3.13 can be considered components under the umbrella Guideline 3.1. However, their importance in ensuring safe food on board ships warrants that they have additional detailed elaboration.

3.2.1 Guideline 3.1: Food safety plans

Guideline 3.1—Food safety plans are in place for each component of the food-chain.

Indicators for Guideline 3.1

An FSP is designed and implemented for:

1. the food source
2. transfer of food to the ship
3. the ship food storage system
4. the ship food preparation and serving system
5. consumer handling and storage processes on board ship.

Guidance notes for Guideline 3.1

Attention should be given to the contemporary use of a preventive, multiple-barrier risk management approach to food safety, termed the FSP, and based around the HACCP principles (as per section 3.1.4).

Most of the microorganisms that cause foodborne disease are killed or inactivated by normal cooking processes. However, there are limitations to those contaminants that can be removed. Cooking processes are not always carried out effectively, and some hazardous agents can persist through cooking processes (e.g. toxins). Furthermore, food can become recontaminated following cooking, either by passengers and crew or by vectors such as rodents and insects. Therefore, reliance should not be placed on the cooking processes alone.

Food poisoning on board ships can be reduced by vendor assurance and careful selection of suppliers, training of food handlers, optimum construction of galleys and strict personal hygiene. Control measures for biological hazards include:

- source control—that is, control of the presence and level of microorganisms by obtaining ingredients from suppliers that can demonstrate adequate controls over the ingredients and suitable transport of the ingredients to ships;
- temperature/time control—that is, proper control of refrigeration and storage time; and proper thawing, cooking and cooling of food. Passenger ship operators should consider alternatives to packed food for takeaway by passengers or eliminate potentially hazardous foods for packaged takeaway, to ensure that these temperature/time control limits are not exceeded;

- cross-contamination control, both direct (e.g. resulting from direct contact between raw and cooked food) and indirect (e.g. resulting from the use of the same utensils to contact both raw and cooked food);
- proper cleaning and disinfection, which can eliminate or reduce levels of microbiological contamination. Galleys should be designed so that the risk of cross-contamination is reduced. Specific guidelines for sanitary conveniences and hand-washing facilities for the shipping industry should be considered by those designing and maintaining ships. Seawater or non-potable water must not be used in or near food or food preparation areas;
- personal and hygienic practices. It is recommended that ships have policies for ensuring that staff with infections that can be transmitted via food do not perform any task connected with food handling. Food handlers with cuts, sores or abrasions on their hands should not handle food unless such sores are treated and covered. Staff should not be penalized for reporting illness; rather, the reporting of illness should be promoted. Preventing outbreaks attributed to infected food handlers requires the cooperation of employers, as many food handlers may conceal infection to avoid pay loss or penalty.

It is important that first-aid boxes are readily available for use in food handling areas and that a suitably trained person is appointed to take charge of first-aid arrangements. There are no specific requirements covering the contents of a first-aid box, but minimum contents might reasonably be a plastic-coated leaflet giving general guidance on first aid, individually wrapped sterile dressings of assorted sizes, sterile eye pads, individually wrapped triangular bandages, safety pins, medium-sized (approximately 12 cm × 12 cm) individually wrapped sterile unmedicated wound dressings and one pair of disposable gloves.

3.2.2 Guideline 3.2: Food receipt

Guideline 3.2—Food is inspected and confirmed to be in safe condition upon receipt.

Indicators for Guideline 3.2

1. Receiving areas/spaces do not harbour hazards.
2. Received food is inspected and confirmed to be in safe condition before acceptance.

Guidance notes for Guideline 3.2

Ship operators are expected to take all practicable measures to ensure that they do not receive unsafe or unsuitable food. This means that they must make sure that the food they receive:

- is protected from contamination;
- is clearly identifiable;
- is at the correct temperature and in the appropriate condition when it arrives (e.g. a food that is labelled frozen and shipped frozen by a food-processing plant shall be received frozen).

Physical facilities of the food receiving area shall:

- have a smooth, non-absorbent and cleanable covering;
- be maintained sound and in good repair, free of chippings, cracks, leakage, seepage, mould, peeling and so forth;
- be free of unused or extraneous materials (cardboard, cloths, papers, sanitizing products, plastic bags, pallets, brooms, etc.);
- be provided with natural or artificial lighting that does not compromise food hygiene, does not change colour and enables good working conditions;
- be provided with electrical wiring installations that are properly covered and insulated;
- be provided with a ventilation system that avoids intense heat, vapour condensation and accumulation of mould, fumes or smoke.

The food receiving area must be cleaned with disinfectant. The disinfectant manufacturer's instructions, including concentration and contact time, shall be followed precisely. The cleaning should take place immediately before food entry.

Food cannot enter by the same area from which solid waste is removed. If it is absolutely impossible to provide different areas, there should be a different schedule, and the area shall always be cleaned before food is received.

Integrated pest management actions shall be implemented at this area according to the provisions established in chapter 7 of this guide.

The Codex Alimentarius provides details of temperatures and conditions that should be confirmed as items are received. A number of examples are given in Table 3-2, although for current requirements, the Codex Alimentarius should be used as the primary source of information.

Table 3-2 Examples of proper food receipt temperatures and conditions for foods supplied to ship

Item	Temperature on receipt	Condition on receipt
Meat and poultry	5 °C or below	Obtained from an approved source; stamped with official inspection stamp Good colour and no odour Packaging clean and in good condition
Seafood	5 °C or below Codex recommends a temperature as close as possible to 0 °C	Obtained from an approved source Good colour and no off-odours Packaging clean and in good condition
Shellfish	7 °C or below Codex recommends a temperature as close as possible to 0 °C	Obtained from approved source Clean, shells closed, no broken shells Shellstock tags must be readable and attached
Crustacea (unprocessed)	7 °C or below	Obtained from an approved source Clean and in good condition
Crustacea (cut or processed)	5 °C or below	Obtained from an approved source Clean and in good condition
Dairy products	5 °C or below unless labelled otherwise	Obtained from an approved source Packaging clean and in good condition
Shell eggs	7 °C or below	Clean and uncracked Obtained from an approved source
Liquid, frozen and dried eggs	5 °C or below	Pasteurized Obtained from an approved source

3.2.3 Guideline 3.3: Equipment and utensils

Guideline 3.3—Equipment and utensils are suitable for food preparation, food storage and contact with food.

Indicator for Guideline 3.3

Equipment and utensils are suitable for food contact and use.

Guidance notes for Guideline 3.3

It is good practice to ensure that the equipment and containers coming into contact with food are designed and constructed to ensure that they can be adequately cleaned, disinfected and maintained to avoid the contamination of food. Equipment and containers must be made of materials with no toxic effect for their intended use. Where necessary, equipment should be durable, movable or capable of being disassembled to allow for maintenance, cleaning and disinfection and to facilitate pest inspection.

Depending on the nature of food operations undertaken, adequate facilities need to be available for preparing, heating, cooling, cooking, refrigerating and freezing food; for monitoring food temperatures; and, when necessary, for controlling ambient temperatures. Equipment used to cook, heat, treat, cool, store or freeze food must be designed to achieve the required food temperatures as rapidly as necessary in the interests of food safety. Such equipment can include design features to allow temperatures to be monitored and controlled.

Containers for waste products and inedible or dangerous substances must be specifically identifiable, suitably constructed and, where appropriate, made of impervious material. Waste containers used in the galley must be provided with foot-operable lids, emptied frequently and easy to clean and disinfect.

All washing facilities, kitchen equipment, storage containers, stoves and hoods used in the preparation and serving of food and all food contact surfaces must be so constructed as to be easily cleaned and disinfected and kept in good repair.

The following is a list of examples of the sort of equipment that might need to be considered and assessed for its suitability:

- blast chillers incorporated into the design of passenger and crew galleys; more than one unit may be necessary depending on the size of the ship, the unit's intended application and the distances between the chillers and the storage and service areas;

- food preparation sinks in as many areas as necessary (i.e. in all meat, fish and vegetable preparation rooms; in cold pantries; and in any other areas where personnel wash or soak food); an automatic vegetable washing machine may be used in addition to food preparation sinks;
- storage cabinets, shelves, racks for food products and equipment in food storage, preparation and service areas, including bars, pantries and storage associated with waiter trays;
- portable tables, carts or pallets in areas where food is dispensed from cooking equipment, such as from soup kettles, steamers, braising pans, tilting skillets or ice storage bins;
- a storage cabinet or rack for large items such as ladles, paddles, whisks and spatulas;
- knife lockers that are easily cleanable and meet food contact standards;
- dish storage and dispensing cabinets;
- food preparation counters that provide sufficient work space;
- drinking fountains;
- cleaning lockers.

Depending on the size of the facilities and the distance to the central pot-washing facilities, heavy-use areas such as bakeries, butcher shops and other preparation areas may require a three-compartment sink with a pre-wash station, or a four-compartment sink with an insert pan and an overhead spray. All food preparation areas are likely to need easy access to a three-compartment utensil-washing sink or a dishwashing machine equipped with a dump sink and a pre-wash hose.

Beverage or condiment dispensing equipment typically requires a readily removable drain pan or built-in drains in the tabletop. Bulk milk dispensers should have readily removable drain pans to enable cleaning of potentially hazardous milk spillages. A utility sink is desirable in areas such as beverage stations where it is necessary to refill pitchers or dispensers or discard liquids such as hot or cold drinks, ice-cream or sherbet. Dipper wells ideally need to be provided with running water and proper drainage.

Clean storage areas need to be sufficient to house all equipment and utensils used in food preparation, such as ladles and cutting blades.

The design of all installed equipment needs to direct food and wash-water drainage into a deck drain scupper or deck sink, and not directly or indirectly onto a deck.

For openings to ice bins, food display cases and other such food and ice holding facilities, tight-fitting doors or similar protective closures are desirable to prevent contamination of stored products.

Countertop openings and rims of food service areas, bains-marie, ice wells and other drop-in type food and ice holding units must be protected with a raised edge or rim of 5 mm or more above the counter level around the opening.

3.2.4 Guideline 3.4: Materials

Guideline 3.4—Materials are suitable for contact with food and protect food from contamination.

Indicators for Guideline 3.4

1. Materials in contact with food are suitable for this purpose.
2. Materials not in contact with food are suitable to their roles in protecting food from contamination.

Guidance notes for Guideline 3.4

1. Food contact areas

The materials used for food contact surfaces need to be suitable—for example, corrosion resistant, non-toxic, non-absorbent, easily cleanable, smooth and durable. This applies especially to heating units in contact with food, cooking fats, oils or similar cooking media. Cutting boards should be of a suitable material, such as one equivalent to or better than hard maple. If using materials other than those already accepted and listed for use as food contact surfaces or containers, advice should be sought from the relevant public health authority before installation. In general, painted surfaces are not recommended for food contact unless appropriate paint is used.

2. Non-food contact areas

Materials used for non-food contact surfaces must be durable and readily cleanable. Welding materials used in joining together non-corrosive materials must be selected to ensure that the weld area is corrosion resistant. Surface coatings and paint should be suitable for their intended use and non-toxic.

All permanent or stationary equipment needs to be installed and constructed with flashing to exclude openings hidden by adjacent structures or other equipment, unless adequate clearance for proper cleaning is provided. As an example, a minimum clearance of 15 cm is recommended under leg-mounted equipment between the lowest horizontal framing member and the deck.

It is important to ensure that counter-mounted equipment, unless portable, is either sealed to the tabletop or mounted on legs. Once again, to facilitate cleaning, counter-mounted equipment should have sufficient clearance, typically at least 7.5 cm, between the lowest horizontal member and the countertop. There is also a need to provide cleaning access behind counter-mounted equipment, including beverage equipment.

The clearance between the back of enclosed equipment, such as ranges and refrigerators, and the bulkhead should be governed by the combined length of the items. For example, for equipment up to 61 cm long, a suitable clearance might be 15 cm; for longer equipment, the clearance might be proportionally greater, up to a maximum of 61 cm for equipment 2.45 m or more in length. If the space between the equipment and the bulkhead is readily accessible from one end, the above clearances could be halved, with 15 cm being a suitable minimum.

If two items of equipment, such as ovens or ranges, are located near each other, the space between them needs to be adequate to enable cleaning. Alternatively, the space between them could be effectively closed on all sides by tightly fitting flashing.

When mounting equipment on a foundation or coaming, an adequate separation distance above the finished deck, at least 10 cm, needs to be provided. Cement or a continuous weld must be used to seal equipment to the foundation. The overhang of the equipment from the foundation must not be excessive, less than 10 cm. To avoid possible vermin habitat, it is advisable to completely seal any overhang of equipment along the bottom.

Equipment installed without adequate clearances, such as those suggested in the previous paragraphs, can have the spaces under, next to and behind them effectively enclosed and sealed to the deck and/or bulkhead. Penetrations such as cable, conduit or pipe openings must be provided with tightly fitting collars made of materials acceptable to the relevant national health administration.

Electrical wiring from permanently installed equipment must be encased in durable and easily cleanable material. The use of braided or woven stainless-steel electrical conduit outside of technical spaces or where it is subject to splash or soiling is not recommended. The length of electrical cords to equipment on benches should be adjusted or the cords fastened in a manner that prevents the cords from lying on countertops.

Other bulkhead- or deckhead-mounted equipment, such as phones, speakers, electrical control panels or outlet boxes, must be sealed to the bulkhead or deckhead panels. Such items must be kept away from areas exposed to food splash.

Any areas where electrical lines, steam pipelines or water pipelines penetrate the panels or tiles of the deck, bulkhead or deckhead, including inside technical spaces or work surfaces, should be tightly sealed. The number of exposed pipelines should be minimized.

3.2.5 Guideline 3.5: Facilities

Guideline 3.5—Facilities are suitable for safe food preparation and serving.

Indicators for Guideline 3.5

1. Water and ice are of potable quality.
2. There are sufficient cleaning and disinfecting facilities.
3. Ventilation is adequate and designed to avoid food contamination.
4. Lighting is sufficient to allow hygienic food operations.
5. Storage facilities are adequate and provide for safe food storage.
6. Food contact areas are sanitary.
7. Non-food contact areas are designed to avoid food contamination.

Guidance notes for Guideline 3.5

1. Water and ice

An adequate supply of potable water with appropriate facilities for its storage and distribution is required to be available whenever necessary to ensure the safety and suitability of food. Non-potable water (e.g. seawater) must have a separate system and must not be supplied to the galley unless essential, as discussed in chapter 2.

Ice that will come in contact with food or drink needs to be manufactured from potable water. Shore sources must be checked with the local health authority, and delivery of ice from shore to ship must be carried out in a sanitary manner. Upon delivery to the ship, shore ice needs to be handled in a sanitary manner, the handler wearing clean clothing, gloves and boots. Ice must be stored in a clean storage room and raised off the surface by use of deck-boards or similar devices permitting drainage and free flow of air. Ice manufactured on board ship needs to be handled and stored in a sanitary manner.

2. Cleaning and disinfecting facilities

To ensure safe food, adequate design criteria must be adopted in constructing systems for cleaning and disinfecting food, utensils, equipment and facilities. Such facilities need an adequate supply of hot and cold potable water.

3. Ventilation

Adequate means of natural or mechanical ventilation help to support safe food operations. Ventilation systems must be designed and constructed so that air does not flow from contaminated areas to clean areas and so that they can be adequately maintained and cleaned. Louvres or vents at ventilation terminals must be readily removable for cleaning. Particular attention should be given to:

- minimizing airborne contamination of food—for example, from aerosols and condensation droplets;
- controlling ambient temperatures;
- where necessary, controlling humidity.

4. Lighting

Adequate natural or artificial lighting supports hygienic work practices. The intensity of light should be set according to the nature of the work. Lighting fixtures should be protected to ensure that food is not contaminated if breakage occurs.

5. Storage

Improper storage of provisions on board seagoing ships is a hazard, as provisions are frequently carried for many weeks or even months, and the ship can be subject to extreme climatic influences. Storage, especially in cold stores, in an unpacked condition might have an adverse effect on provisions.

The type of storage facilities required will depend on the nature of the food on board. Adequate facilities for the storage of food, ingredients and non-food chemicals (e.g. cleaning materials, lubricants and fuels) must be provided. Food storage facilities must be designed and constructed to:

- permit adequate maintenance and cleaning;
- avoid pest access and harbourage;
- enable food to be effectively protected from contamination during storage;
- provide an environment that minimizes the deterioration of food (e.g. by temperature and humidity control).

6. Food contact areas

Food contact surfaces should be free of open seams, cracks or crevices and easily cleaned. Exposed construction fittings (e.g. bolts and nuts) are not generally acceptable. Corners formed by joining the sides of food contact surfaces must be built with a radius of curvature that helps cleaning, at least 3 mm. On coved corners of food contact surfaces, the coved radius must be sufficient to help cleaning, at least 1.6 mm.

Food areas need to be protected against the leakage or seepage of lubricants or other extraneous or foreign substances. Sound deadening or undercoating material is not generally applied to the surface of equipment that is directly above an area where exposed food is kept, as this material may harbour hazards.

Drawers and bins that come into contact with food must be removable and easily cleaned. They must be free of open seams or cracks and finished smooth on all sides. Covers, insets or receptacles for unpackaged food or beverages must be removable or designed for easy cleaning in situ.

7. Suitable non-food contact areas

Exposed non-food contact surfaces should be designed to reduce risks of contaminating food by being free of open seams, cracks or crevices. Equipment housing or component parts must be made free of openings into inaccessible areas where food, liquid or dust may enter and insects may shelter. Mixers, refrigerators, compressors and similar units, if provided with openings or louvres, should contain readily removable inspection ports or panels, with routine cleaning in place.

Deck-mounted equipment must be installed with the base flush with the deck (openings and joints sealed) or with a minimum clearance of 15 cm between the lowest horizontal framing member of the equipment and the deck. This also applies when equipment is mounted on an island or curbing. Control mechanisms, couplings and other components mounted on the housing of the equipment must be designed and installed to preclude the entrance of dirt and vermin and the formation of inaccessible areas, which may prevent proper cleaning and inspection. Bases, curbs or elevated islands for supporting equipment above deck level, if provided with toe space, must not be indented a distance greater than the height of the lowest framing member of the equipment above the deck. Toe space should have a minimum suitable height of 5 cm. Enclosed spaces, such as columns, vertical supports and legs, must be sealed against the entrance of vermin.

Horizontal openings on top of food storage cabinets must be protected by a coaming around their periphery. The minimum height of this coaming needs to be 5 mm, measured from the surface of the cabinet or from the overflow level. Openings in work tables or dish tables to food refuse and waste receptacles can have a watertight turned-down edge extending at least 1.25 cm below the table surface, unless the opening is provided with a scrap block. Exposed edges on horizontal surfaces, such as tops of dressers, tables and shelves, can have turned-down or return flanges with a suitable space of at least 2 cm between the sheared edge and the frame angles, or they should be totally enclosed.

Hoods over steam kettles, ranges and other cooking units should have smooth, easily cleanable interiors. Gutters, if provided, must be designed and dimensioned to facilitate cleaning. Filters, if used, must be installed to direct condensation into gutters. Baffles, vanes, dampers and other air-control facilities must be readily accessible or removable. Sea-rails on cooking ranges must be removable and easily cleaned.

Exposed refrigerant coils located in food compartments must be of a finless type and arranged to allow thorough cleaning. Blower-type or fin-type evaporators must be enclosed or shielded to protect them from spillage of food and to protect the food from condensation. Enclosed-type refrigeration evaporators must be provided with condensate drains. Refrigerant and water coils in water-cooling units must be readily accessible for brush cleaning and have the ability to be flushed and drained.

Sliding doors on galley and pantry equipment must be removable and their tracks free of inaccessible openings. The lower tracks must be slotted at the ends to facilitate removal of dust and debris. Equipment doors, whether sliding or hinged, should avoid openings into inaccessible areas. If gaskets are used on insulated doors, they must be easily cleanable and replaceable and should fit tightly. Door catches and other fastening devices must be made free of openings that could permit vermin and debris to enter channels, door panels or other component parts of the equipment. Catches, hinges and other hardware must be fabricated of smooth, easily cleanable material.

Cutting boards must be readily removable for cleaning or easily cleanable without removal. They must be free of open seams or cracks and finished smooth on all sides. Drawers and bins must be readily removable and easily cleanable.

Insulation material must be protected against seepage and condensation. Flashing must be made to exclude food fragments or debris.

Coaming around equipment such as steam kettles must be sealed against seepage, infiltration and the entrance of vermin and provided with drains having removable strainers. The drain must be located at the lowest point within the area. Drains for galley and sink equipment should have the following dimensions:

- sinks: 3.75 cm minimum diameter
- steam tables and bains-marie: 2.5 cm minimum diameter.

Exposed horizontal drainpipes, including the traps, must be installed to permit proper cleaning of the floor area. Drainpipes should not be located above areas used for storage, preparation or serving of food.

To help avoid contamination, water inlets to steam tables, kettles and other sink-type equipment must be located a minimum safe distance of twice the diameter of the water inlet, and in any case not less than 2.5 cm, above the flood-level rim. If the water supply line is required to be below that, vacuum breakers of an acceptable type should be properly installed.

Shelves used as false bottoms must be readily removable or sealed in place to preclude the entrance of food fragments and vermin. Silverware containers must be removable and designed and fabricated to permit cleaning followed by disinfection or sterilization. Dipper wells for ice-cream dippers must be equipped with running water from an above-the-rim inlet and constructed of smooth, seamless material.

3.2.6 Guideline 3.6: Storage, preparation and service spaces

Guideline 3.6—Spaces are suitable for the safe storage, preparation and service of food.

Indicators for Guideline 3.6

1. Spaces are readily cleaned and disinfected and do not harbour hazards.
2. Temperatures used in storage do not support microbial pathogen growth.
3. Ready-to-eat food is separated from raw food.
4. All food is separated and protected from sources of contamination.

The decks, or flooring, of all spaces where food or drink is stored, handled and prepared, or where utensils are cleaned and stored, must be so constructed as to be easily cleaned, maintained and inspected at all times. Surfaces must be smooth and kept in good repair.

To comply with good practice, provision rooms, walk-in refrigerators and freezers and transportation corridors should use hard, durable, non-absorbent decking (e.g. tiles or diamond-plate corrugated stainless-steel deck panels in refrigerated provision rooms). Painted steel decking is acceptable in provision passageways and drystore areas, although stainless steel is preferred. It is advisable to provide tight-fitting stainless-steel bulkheads in walk-in refrigerators and freezers, and to line doors with stainless steel. Painted steel is acceptable for provision passageways and in drystore areas. Light colours are recommended to reveal any dirt. If a forklift will be used in these areas, reinforced stainless-steel panels should be used so that buckling is prevented, and bumper guards should be fitted on bulkheads to prevent damage. It is good practice to close deckhead-mounted cable trays, piping or other difficult-to-clean deckhead-mounted equipment or completely close the deckhead. All bulkhead and deck junctures should be coved (e.g. a 10 mm radius) and sealed tight.

For galleys, food preparation rooms and pantries, decks should be constructed from hard, durable, non-absorbent and non-skid material. Installation can include durable coving with adequate radius, at least 10 mm, or open design, such as greater than 90 degrees, as an integral part of the deck and bulkhead interface and at the juncture between decks and equipment foundations. Stainless steel or other coving, if installed, must be of sufficient thickness to be durable, and stainless-steel deck plate panels must be sealed with a continuous, non-corroding weld. All deck tiling must be sealed with a durable, watertight grouting material.

In technical spaces below under-counter cabinets, counters or refrigerators, the deck must be a durable, non-absorbent, easily cleanable surface, such as tile or stainless steel. Painted steel or concrete decking is not recommended. All openings where piping and other items penetrate through the deck must be sealed. Bulkheads and deckheads, including doors, door frames and columns, must be constructed with a high-quality, corrosion-resistant stainless steel. The gauge should be thick enough that the panels do not warp, flex or separate under normal conditions. For seams greater than 1 mm but less than 3 mm that must be sealed, it is common practice to use an appropriate sealant. For bulkhead and deckhead seams too large to be so sealed (greater than 3 mm), stainless-steel profile strips are recommended. All bulkheads to which equipment is attached need to be of sufficient thickness or reinforcement to allow for the reception of fasteners or welding without compromising the quality and construction of the panels. Utility line connections need to be installed through a stainless steel or other easily cleanable food service–approved conduit that is mounted away from bulkheads for ease in cleaning. Backsplash attachments need to be sealed to the bulkhead with a continuous or tack weld and polish. An appropriate sealant is required to make the backsplash attachment watertight. All openings must be sealed where piping and other items penetrate the bulkheads and deckheads, including inside technical compartments.

For food service areas, it is advisable to ensure that all buffet lines have hard, durable, non-absorbent decks that are a suitable width, at least 1 m, measured from the edge of the service counter or from the outside edge of the tray rail. The dining-room service stations can have a hard, durable, non-absorbent deck (e.g. sealed granite or marble), with a safe separation distance of at least 61 cm from the edge of the working sides of the service station. The decks behind service counters, under equipment and in technical spaces must be constructed of hard, durable, non-absorbent materials (e.g. tiles, epoxy resin or stainless steel). Painted steel or concrete decking is not recommended. Durable coving with radius at least 10 mm or open design greater than 90 degrees must be used as an integral part of the deck and bulkhead interface and at the juncture between decks and equipment foundations. Stainless-steel or other coving, if installed, needs to be of sufficient thickness to be durable and securely installed. Durable linoleum tile or vinyl deck covering is recommended only in staff, crew or officers' dining areas. Bulkheads and deckheads may be constructed of decorative tiles, pressed metal panels or other hard, durable, non-corroding materials. Stainless steel is not required in these areas. However, the materials used need to be easily cleanable. All openings where piping and other items penetrate through the deck need to be sealed.

Bulkheads and deckheads of spaces in which food and drink are stored, prepared or handled, or in which utensils are stored or cleaned, should have smooth, hard-finished, light-coloured, washable surfaces. Fibrous insulation or similar materials must be sheathed to prevent particles of the insulating materials from falling on foods. Cloth or plaster surfacing is not generally acceptable for satisfactory protection. Fibrous air filters are not recommended to be installed in the deckheads or over food processing equipment. Perforated acoustic material is not recommended in galleys, pantries, sculleries and other food handling or food storage spaces. It is acceptable for use in dining-rooms, provided that the particles of material are prevented from falling on food through holes and seams.

Pipes in unsheathed deckheads over spaces where food is stored, handled, prepared or served, or where utensils are washed, must be insulated if condensation forms. Drainage lines carrying sewage or other liquid waste should be diverted from passing directly over or horizontally through spaces where food is prepared, served or stored, or where utensils are washed. Where such drainage lines exist, they must not contain clean-out plugs and flanges, or these should be welded closed where they must occur. Exceptions in existing installations may be made where the lines do not leak, drip or spray non-potable liquids on food or utensils. Drainpipes passing through insulation surrounding refrigerated spaces are considered acceptable.

3.2.7 Guideline 3.7: Toilet and personal hygiene facilities

Guideline 3.7—There are adequate toilet and personal hygiene facilities for food handling personnel.

Indicators for Guideline 3.7

1. There are adequate and suitably located toilets for food handling personnel.
2. There are adequate and suitably located hand-washing and hand-drying facilities for food handling personnel.

Guidance notes for Guideline 3.7

1. Toilet facilities

Adequate toilet facilities for food handling personnel must be placed near food preparation spaces to encourage personal hygiene and sanitation. On smaller ships, these facilities may be shared by the crew. Such facilities need to be accessible at all times. To avoid contamination, toilet rooms should not open directly into spaces where food is prepared, stored or served. If toilet rooms do open directly into such food areas, the doors need to be tight-fitting and self-closing. Wherever possible, there should be a ventilated space between the toilet rooms and food spaces.

Adequate hand-washing and hand-drying facilities must be provided within or adjacent to toilet rooms. Toilet rooms should include hot and cold running water from a single mixing outlet, single-service paper or cloth-towel dispenser, suitable soap or detergent and signs over the basin reading, for example, "WASH HANDS AFTER USING TOILET—WASH BASIN BEFORE AND AFTER USING". Signs requiring personnel to wash hands after using the toilet should also be conspicuously posted on the bulkhead adjacent to the door of the toilet.

The following areas can also be provided with similar hand-washing facilities, with appropriate signs located above basins:

- main galley: additional washbasins may be needed, depending on distance, partitions, size of spaces, number of employees served and other impediments to convenient use of facilities;
- individual galleys, pantries, bakery spaces, butcher spaces, vegetable preparation rooms and sculleries: a single washbasin may serve more than one such area if easily accessible.

Where a common washbasin serves both a food handling space and a toilet for food handlers, a sign reading as above must be posted. On ships where hand-washing facilities exist in a food service employees' stateroom, easily accessible from the food handling spaces, additional facilities are not required in the food handling spaces. In such cases, individual cloth towels for food handlers are acceptable. Scullery sinks, slop sinks, laundry tubs, dishwashing sinks and similar facilities cannot be used for hand washing. Wash water may be used at washbasins provided that the water is heated to a temperature of 77 °C. Only potable water should be used for the cold-water supply to washbasins.

Facilities need to be readily available to encourage appropriate personal hygiene and to avoid food contamination. Facilities to be located beside the galley can include:

- adequate means of hygienically washing and drying hands, including washbasins and a supply of hot and cold water;
- toilets of appropriate hygienic design with handbasins, which do not open directly into galleys or other food handling areas;
- an adequate supply of soap and hand-drying facilities at handbasins;
- adequate changing facilities for personnel, including suitable storage facilities for clothes.

3.2.8 Guideline 3.8: Dishwashing

Guideline 3.8—There are adequate and effective dishwashing facilities.

Indicators for Guideline 3.8

1. Dishwashing facilities are adequate and suitable for safe and effective dishwashing.
2. Waste arising from dishwashing does not recontaminate wash water.

Guidance notes for Guideline 3.8

1. Dishwashing facilities

Rinse hoses for pre-washing are recommended in some areas. If a sink is to be used for pre-rinsing, a removable strainer may be needed.

All dishwashing machine components, including encased pulper wiring, must be elevated at least 15 cm above the deck to provide for drainage.

Removable stainless-steel splash panels must be provided to protect the pulper and technical areas. Grinder cones, pulper tables and dish landing tables must be constructed from stainless steel with continuous welding. Platforms for supporting dishwashing equipment must be constructed from stainless steel, avoiding the use of painted steel.

Dishwashing machines must be designed and sized for their intended use and installed according to the manufacturer's recommendations. Dishwashing machines using chemical sanitizers must be equipped with a device that indicates audibly or visually when more chemical sanitizer needs to be added.

Dishwashing machines can have easily accessible and readable data plates affixed. The plate can include the machine's design and operating specifications:

- temperatures required for washing, rinsing and sanitizing;
- pressure required for the freshwater sanitizing rinse, unless the machine is designed to use only a pumped sanitizing rinse;
- conveyor speed for conveyor machines or cycle time for stationary rack machines;
- chemical concentration (if chemical sanitizers are used).

Three-compartment dishwashing sinks with a separate pre-wash station must be provided for the main galley, crew galley, lido galley and other full-service galleys with pot-washing areas. For meat, fish and vegetable preparation areas, there must be at least one three-compartment sink or an automatic dishwashing machine with a pre-wash station. Sinks must be large enough to submerge the largest piece of equipment used in the area. Sinks should have coved, continuously welded, internal corners. Dishwashing machine wash and rinse tanks should be equipped with baffles, curtains or other means to minimize internal cross-contamination of the solutions in wash and rinse tanks. A pass-through type dishwashing machine is preferable to an under-counter model.

Hot-water sanitizing sinks (accept those that use halogen for the sanitization step) must be equipped with accessible and easily readable thermometers, a long-handled stainless-steel wire basket or other retrieval system and a jacketed or coiled steam supply with a temperature-control valve to control water temperature.

Sufficient shelving for storage of soiled and clean ware must be provided. As an example, the storage available for soiled ware must be approximately one third the volume provided for clean ware. Either solid or open tubular shelving or racks must be used. Solid overhead shelves must be designed so that they drain at each end to the landing table below.

Adequate ventilation is required to prevent condensation on the deckhead or adjacent bulkheads. Any filters installed over dishwashing equipment need to be easily removed for cleaning.

2. Food waste handling

In all food preparation areas, adequate space is needed for trash cans, garbage grinders or pulping systems. Food waste grinders are optional in pantries and bars.

For tables that store used and soiled dishes and that are installed with pulper systems, the pulper trough needs to extend the full length of the table and slope towards the pulper to help take away waste. The table's back edge must be sealed to the bulkhead or have sufficient clearance, 45 cm, between the table and the bulkhead. Such tables must be designed to drain waste liquids and to prevent contamination of adjacent surfaces.

To prevent water from pooling, clean tables should be equipped with across-the-counter gutters with drains at the exit from the machine and sloped to the scupper. A second gutter and drain line must be installed if the first gutter does not effectively remove pooled water from the entire table. The length of drain lines must be minimized and, where possible, drain lines must be placed in straight vertical lines with no angles.

One of the following arrangements must be used to prevent excessive contamination of rinse water with wash-water splash:

- an across-the-counter gutter with a drain dividing the wash compartment from the rinse compartment;
- a splash shield of sufficient height, greater than 10 cm, above the flood-level rim of the sink between the wash and rinse compartments;
- an overflow drain in the wash compartment sufficiently, at least 10 cm, below the flood level.

3.2.9 Guideline 3.9: Safe food storage

Guideline 3.9—There are safe food storage systems.

Indicators for Guideline 3.9

1. Temperatures used in storage do not support microbial pathogen growth.
2. Ready-to-eat food is separated from raw food.
3. All food is separated and protected from sources of contamination.

Guidance notes for Guideline 3.9

1. Temperature

Inadequate food temperature control is one of the most common causes of foodborne illness and food spoilage on ships. On passenger ships, the preparation of a wide variety of foods, at the same time, for a large number of people increases the risk of food mishandling and unsatisfactory temperature variations. For example, an outbreak of staphylococcal food poisoning on a cruise ship occurred after pastry was prepared in large quantities by several food handlers. This provided opportunities for the introduction of staphylococci into the pastry. Prolonged time at warm temperature allowed for production of enterotoxin.

In large-scale catering, it is often necessary to prepare food hours before it is needed and to hold food under refrigeration, in a hot holding apparatus or even at ambient temperature. If procedures are strictly controlled and storage temperatures are at levels that will not permit bacterial growth, hazards can be adequately controlled. The ship's operators must implement systems to ensure that temperature is controlled effectively where it is critical to the safety and suitability of food. Where appropriate, temperature-recording devices must be checked at regular intervals and tested for accuracy by the crew.

The temperature within refrigerators and freezers should be measured using an internal thermometer. Sufficient shelving is needed in all refrigeration units to prevent stacking and to permit adequate ventilation and cleaning. Examples of suitable food storage temperatures are found in documents of the Vessel Sanitation Program of the United States Centers for Disease Control and Prevention and the Codex Alimentarius Commission that specifically relate to the storage of food on passenger and cruise ships. These documents are subject to periodic review, and current versions should be considered by the ship's operator.

When foods, particularly large joints of meat or poultry, are undercooked or inadequately thawed, with cooking times too short and temperatures too low, *Salmonella* and other bacteria may survive. Subsequent poor storage will permit multiplication of organisms and the introduction of a significant risk. It is important that large joints of meat and poultry are thawed out before cooking. Precautions need to be taken to cool cooked food quickly and to cold-store those items that will not be cooked immediately.

2. Separation of raw and ready-to-eat food

Pathogens can be transferred from one food to another, either by direct contact or by food handlers, contact surfaces or airborne transmission. Space is sometimes limited in galleys, preventing the clear separation of raw and cooked foods.

Raw food, especially meat, needs to be effectively separated, either physically or by time, from ready-to-eat foods, with effective intermediate cleaning and, where appropriate, disinfection. Surfaces, utensils, equipment, fixtures and fittings must be thoroughly cleaned and, where necessary, disinfected after raw food has been handled.

3. Separation of food from contaminant sources

Systems must be in place to prevent contamination of foods by foreign bodies such as glass or metal shards from machinery, dust, harmful fumes and unwanted chemicals, particularly after any maintenance work.

3.2.10 Guideline 3.10: Maintenance, cleaning and disinfection

Guideline 3.10—There is a comprehensive maintenance, cleaning and disinfection programme.

Indicator for Guideline 3.10

1. There is a comprehensive maintenance, cleaning and disinfection programme.

Guidance notes for Guideline 3.10

Maintenance, cleaning and disinfection programmes ensure that all parts of the establishment are appropriately clean and include the cleaning of cleaning equipment. Cleaning and disinfection programmes must be continually and effectively monitored for their suitability and effectiveness and, where necessary, documented.

Cleaning can remove food residues and dirt, which may be a source of contamination. The necessary cleaning methods will depend on the nature of the catering and size of the ship. Disinfection may be necessary after cleaning. Cleaning chemicals should be handled and used carefully and in accordance with manufacturers' instructions. Cleaning chemicals should be stored, separately from food, in clearly identified containers to avoid the risk of contamination. Galley and food areas and equipment need to be kept in an appropriate state of repair and condition to:

- facilitate all cleaning and disinfection procedures
- function as intended, particularly at critical steps
- prevent contamination of food (e.g. from debris and chemicals).

Cleaning must be carried out by physical methods, such as heat, scrubbing, turbulent flow, vacuum cleaning or other methods that avoid the use of water; or chemical methods, using detergents, alkalis or acids; or by a combination of physical and chemical methods. Cleaning procedures may involve:

- removing gross debris from surfaces
- applying a detergent solution to loosen soil and bacterial film
- rinsing with potable water to remove loosened soil and residues of detergent
- disinfecting, where necessary.

Where written cleaning programmes are used, they might specify:

- areas, equipment and utensils to be cleaned
- cleaning materials, equipment and chemicals to be used

- who is responsible for particular tasks
- methods, including the dismantling and reassembly of equipment
- safety precautions
- frequency of cleaning and monitoring arrangements
- the standard(s) to be achieved.

In addition, there may at times be deep cleaning, such as at six-month or annual intervals, subject to usage and requirements of the specific area (e.g. ducting and extraction systems). Cleaning programmes might also be in place for environmental cleaning, with appropriate methods for cleaning the cleaning materials.

During pesticide spraying, all foodstuffs, utensils, and food preparation and cleansing equipment should be covered to protect them from toxic substances. Instructions for the use of sprays should be carefully followed (refer to chapter 7).

3.2.11 Guideline 3.11: Personal hygiene

Guideline 3.11—Food handling personnel practise good personal hygiene.

Indicators for Guideline 3.11

1. All food handlers should practise good personal hygiene.
2. Food handlers known to be infected with potentially hazardous conditions are not permitted to handle food.

Guidance notes for Guideline 3.11

Crew, including maintenance personnel, who do not maintain an appropriate degree of personal cleanliness, or who have certain illnesses or conditions, can contaminate food and transmit illness to consumers.

1. Food handler hygiene

Food handlers need to maintain a high degree of personal cleanliness and, where appropriate, wear suitable protective clothing, head coverings and footwear. Cuts and wounds, where personnel are permitted to continue working, must be covered by suitable waterproof dressings.

Protective clothing should be light coloured, without external pockets and not one-piece overalls, as these could become contaminated from the floor when using the toilet. Disposable gloves might be used in some food handling situations; however, they can be misused and give food handlers a false sense of hygiene security.

Personnel need to wash their hands to ensure food safety, such as:

- at the start of food handling activities;
- immediately after using the toilet;
- after handling raw food or any contaminated material, where this could result in contamination of other food items.

People engaged in food handling activities should avoid handling ready-to-eat food and refrain from behaviour that could result in contamination of food, such as:

- handling money
- smoking
- spitting
- chewing or eating
- sneezing or coughing over unprotected food.

Personal effects such as jewellery, watches, pins or other items must not be worn or brought into food handling areas if they pose a threat to food safety.

2. Food handler illness

Crew known, or suspected, to be suffering from or carrying a disease or illness likely to be transmitted through food should not be allowed to enter any food handling areas if there is a likelihood of them contaminating food. Any person affected needs to immediately report the illness or symptoms. In one outbreak of foodborne viral gastroenteritis, six food handlers were ill, but they were reluctant to report their infections because of concerns about job security. The outbreak investigation implicated freshly cut fruit salad at two buffets. This is a difficult issue to resolve, because food handlers may deny that they are ill for fear of being penalized. Even when symptoms of illness have abated, people can remain infectious, or symptoms may reappear. Therefore, food handlers should ideally not begin working with food for at least 48 hours following the cessation of symptoms. In practice, this recommendation is purely practical, as people can remain infectious for weeks, albeit at a reduced level. Therefore, recently ill food handlers should be encouraged to take extra precautions.

Conditions that should be reported to management so that the need for medical examination and/or possible exclusion from food handling can be considered include:

- jaundice
- diarrhoea

- vomiting
- fever
- sore throat with fever
- coughing
- visibly infected skin lesions (boils, cuts, etc.)
- discharges from the ear, eye or nose.

New food handling staff must be asked questions about their state of health, and all food handling staff must be asked about their state of health after a period of leave. Possible questions include those found in *Regulatory guidance and best practice advice for food business operators* (United Kingdom Food Standards Agency, 2009), which provides questions to ask employees when considering employing new food handlers or reinstating food handlers after any extended shore leave.

3.2.12 Guideline 3.12: Training

Guideline 3.12—Food handlers are adequately trained in food safety.

Indicator for Guideline 3.12

1. There is a comprehensive food handler training programme.

Guidance notes for Guideline 3.12

Those engaged in food preparation or who come directly or indirectly into contact with food need to be trained and/or instructed in food hygiene to a level appropriate to the operations they are to perform.

Food hygiene training is fundamentally important. All personnel need to be aware of their role and responsibilities in protecting food from contamination or deterioration. Food handlers need to have the necessary knowledge and skills to enable them to handle food hygienically. Those who handle strong cleaning chemicals or other potentially hazardous chemicals must be instructed in safe handling techniques. This includes maintenance personnel who enter food handling areas in order to undertake their work. It is not essential that such employees are trained in all food hygiene matters, but they should have an awareness of the relevant hygiene aspects appropriate to their work.

Periodic assessments of the effectiveness of training and instruction programmes must be made, as well as routine supervision and checks to ensure that procedures are being carried out effectively.

Managers and supervisors of food processes need to have the necessary knowledge of food hygiene principles and practices to be able to judge potential risks and take the necessary action to remedy deficiencies. More advanced training courses should deal with management and systems, including HACCP.

3.2.13 Guideline 3.13: Food wastes

Guideline 3.13—Food waste is stored and disposed of in a hygienic manner.

Indicator for Guideline 3.13

1. Food waste is managed to prevent contamination of food and to prevent vermin proliferation.

Guidance notes for Guideline 3.13

Food wastes and refuse readily attract rodents and vermin, particularly flies and cockroaches. The proper retention, storage and disposal of such wastes on board, ashore and overboard where shore areas will not be affected will prevent the creation of health hazards and public nuisances.

All ships must be equipped with facilities for safe storage of food refuse. All food refuse must be received and stored in watertight, non-absorbent and easily cleaned containers, fitted with tight covers that should be closed during food preparation and serving and cleaning operations in food handling spaces. These containers must be placed in waste storage spaces, specifically constructed and used for this purpose, or on open decks when necessary. After emptying, each container must be thoroughly scrubbed, washed and treated with disinfectant, if necessary, to prevent odours and to minimize the attraction of rodents, flies and cockroaches. Containers should not be left uncovered except during the necessary food handling and cleanup procedures.

It is important to characterize the waste stream and the amount of wastes produced in galleys and related areas to provide a basis for planning to prevent environmental contamination. People in charge of waste collection should use personal protection equipment, including special disposable gloves, face masks and/or protective eyewear, safety boots and appropriate protective clothing.

4 Recreational water environments

4.1 Background

This chapter focuses on waterborne disease arising from recreational water environments on cruise ships. A previous chapter (chapter 2) considered disease associated with potable water supplied on board.

Swimming pools and similar recreational water environments may be located either outdoors or indoors, or both. They may be supplied with potable or marine water, supervised or unsupervised and heated or unheated. For the purposes of this guide, swimming pools, hot tubs, whirlpools, spa pools and plunge pools are considered together under the general heading of recreational water environments.

4.1.1 Health risks associated with recreational water environments on ships

Recreational water environments can present a number of risks to health. The most immediate and severe danger arises from accidental drowning. Another source of harm is injuries, potentially serious or even fatal, that can arise from slipping and tripping or from becoming snagged in ropes and fences or fittings such as ladders and drains. There have even been cases where swimmers have been thrown clear of the pool onto hard surfaces in heavy seas. In relation to ship sanitation, a number of infectious diseases can be acquired in swimming and spa pools that can cause diarrhoea or skin, ear, eye and upper respiratory infections. Hot tubs and whirlpools and associated equipment can create an ideal habitat for the proliferation of *Legionella* and *Mycobacterium* spp. In addition, *Pseudomonas aeruginosa* is frequently present in whirlpools, and skin infections have been reported when pool design or management is poor.

Pathogens transmitted by the faecal–oral route have commonly been associated with swimming and spa pools. Contamination occurs when pathogens enter with human sewage or animal faecal contamination or are released directly by infected bathers. One of the most important such pathogens is *Cryptosporidium* spp., which have infectious oocysts that are resistant to even the highest levels of chlorine that are generally used for maintaining residual disinfection in pools. Thousands of cases of swimming-associated cryptosporidiosis have been reported (Lemmon, McAnulty & Bawden-Smith, 1996; United States Centers for Disease Control and Prevention, 2001a), and public swimming pools can be temporarily shut down as a result. Where water quality and treatment have been inadequate, bacterial infections from *Shigella* spp. (United States Centers for Disease Control and Prevention, 2001b) and *Escherichia coli* O157:H7 (United States Centers for Disease Control and Prevention, 1996) have been associated with swimming and spa pools.

Infections of surfaces such as skin and ears have been associated with spa pools where disinfection has been inadequate. These infections arise from opportunistic pathogens that are commonly present in water and soils. The recreational water environment presents a considerable risk because it can both amplify the concentration of the hazard and facilitate exposure of humans. The presence of organic matter and elevated temperatures associated with many recreational water environments can provide an environment suitable for the proliferation of opportunistic pathogens that can infect mucous membranes, lungs, skin and wounds. The loss of disinfectant residual in these environments will permit proliferation of such pathogens to unsafe levels.

Pseudomonas aeruginosa infection has been associated with a number of skin and ear infections arising from immersion in water with inadequate disinfection (Gustafson et al., 1983; Ratnam et al., 1986; United States Centers for Disease Control and Prevention, 2000). Symptoms include outer ear and ear canal infections ("swimmer's ear" or otitis externa) and skin infections such as dermatitis and folliculitis. Where aerosols are generated, the elevated temperature found in some recreational water environments can support *Legionella* spp., which have caused outbreaks of legionnaires' disease associated with hot tubs, including outbreaks on board ships discussed in the review by Rooney et al. (2004). More recently, mycobacterial infections have been associated with pneumonitis linked to exposure to aerosols from swimming and spa pools (Falkinham, 2003).

In using disinfectants, risk from microbial hazards can arise. For example, harm can result from excessive disinfectant chemical addition either directly or potentially through disinfection by-products. The disinfection by-products arise when chlorine reacts with organic matter, such as is found in sloughed skin, sweat and urine, and forms organohalide compounds, such as chloroform. Ozone can also react to produce a different set of by-products. These by-product compounds are of uncertain health significance at the low concentrations found, but might be weakly associated with certain types of cancer or adverse pregnancy outcomes if consumed or inhaled in large amounts over extended periods of time (WHO, 2011).

Usage levels of recreational water environments are directly related to risk. The more people that recreate, the higher the concentrations of pathogens released, the greater the demand on the disinfection system and the higher the number of people in a position to become infected.

Pools are particularly attractive to children and infants, which in turn gives rise to an increased risk of contamination and an increased risk to safety. Children and infants are more likely than adults to swallow pool water and be infected with enteric pathogens, and they are more likely to release faeces into the water, either through smears or through accidental faecal release (AFR). Finally, children and infants are more prone than adults to carelessness and slips, trips and drowning.

Another important risk factor that particularly affects pools on ships is the movement of the ship itself. This movement increases the likelihood of accidents in particular.

4.1.2 Recreational water environment guidelines

The *Guidelines for safe recreational water environments, volume 2, Swimming pools and similar environments* (WHO, 2006) should be referred to, as these apply generally to recreational water environments. Attention should be given to the contemporary use of a preventive, multiple-barrier risk management approach to recreational water safety (WHO, 2006).

4.2 Guidelines

This section provides user-targeted information and guidance, identifying responsibilities and providing examples of practices that can control risks. Three specific *guidelines* (situations to aim for and maintain) are presented, each of which is accompanied by a set of *indicators* (measures for whether the guidelines are met) and *guidance notes* (advice on applying the guidelines and indicators in practice, highlighting the most important aspects that need to be considered when setting priorities for action).

4.2.1 Guideline 4.1: Design and operation

Guideline 4.1—Pools are designed and operated in ways that reduce risks to safe levels.

Indicators for Guideline 4.1

1. Circulation and hydraulics ensure adequate mixing to enable disinfection.
2. A realistic bather load is catered for in the design.
3. Filtration is designed to remove oocysts and cysts.
4. Disinfection is designed to inactivate pathogens.
5. *Legionella* bacteria are controlled through the use of biocides and water turnover.
6. Ventilation is designed to maintain air quality within the indoor recreational water environment.

Guidance notes for Guideline 4.1

Outbreaks associated with recreational water environments have been linked to poor system design. Therefore, the first disease prevention strategy is ensuring the adequate design of recreational water environments given the extent and nature of use. Another common cause of outbreaks is improper operation of controls, such as allowing recreational water environments to be bunkered beyond capacity or engaging in poor operational practices. Design limits should be adhered to and systems should be properly operated at all times.

Treatment systems can reduce contamination levels, but these can become overloaded. Therefore, reliance should not be placed on treatment alone, and multiple barriers should be actively maintained, including:

- filling and topping up recreational water environments with the safest possible water;
- controlling usage rates to within system design capacity by managing bather load;
- maintaining treatment to control forms of contamination;
- taking prompt action to clear the recreational water environment in the event of an incident and remove overt contamination, such as visible faecal releases.

Pool design needs to be tailored to a realistic understanding of the way in which the pool will be used. For example, the number and type of users, the temperature of use and any special health considerations for particular user groups will all affect the details of how the pool should be designed, constructed and managed. Specific considerations might include:

- the daily opening hours
- the peak periods of use
- the anticipated number of users
- special requirements, such as temperature and equipment.

Swimming-pool and bathing-pool water needs to be safe. These water quality requirements need to be met through optimal matching of the following design factors:

- design of the correct pool hydraulics (to ensure optimal distribution of disinfectant throughout the pool);
- adequate circulation in recirculating swimming pools, such as complete circulation of the water within the pool, with replacement of the water every 6 hours or less during pool operation;
- installation of the appropriate treatment system (to remove particulate pollutants and disinfectant-resistant microorganisms);
- installation of a disinfection system (to inactivate infectious microorganisms so that the water cannot transmit and propagate disease-causing microbial agents);
- inclusion of systems to add fresh water at frequent intervals (to dilute substances that cannot be removed from the water by treatment).

Control of pathogens is typically achieved by a combination of recirculation of pool water through treatment (typically involving some form of filtration plus disinfection) and the application of a residual disinfectant to inactivate microorganisms introduced to the pool by bathers.

A dedicated crew member should be assigned to the operation of the recreational water environment and should be suitably trained.

A. Swimming pools

The pool and its water supply need to be designed, constructed and operated in view of the health and safety protection of bathers. These design, construction and operational issues are summarized in the paragraphs below, and details on specific requirements of various pool and spa types follow.

1. Circulation and hydraulics

The purpose of paying close attention to circulation and hydraulics is to ensure that the whole pool is adequately served. Treated water needs to reach all parts of the pool, and polluted water needs to be removed—especially from areas most used and most polluted by bathers. If not, even good water treatment may not result in good water quality. The design and positioning of inlets, outlets and surface water withdrawal are crucial.

Pools usually use seawater or a potable water supply passing through an air gap or backflow preventer. The fill level of the pool is at the skim gutter level. The pool overflows can either be directed by gravity to the make-up tank for recirculation through the filter system or disposed of as waste. Surface skimmers need to be capable of handling sufficient volume, such as approximately 80%, of the filter flow of the recirculation system. There should be sufficient skimmers, such as at least one skimmer for each 47 m^2 of pool surface area.

Circulation rate is related to turnover period, which is the time taken for a volume of water equivalent to the entire pool water volume to pass through the filters and treatment plant and back to the pool. In principle, the shorter the turnover period, the more frequent the pool water treatment. Turnover periods need to suit the particular type of pool. Ideally, turnover must be designed to vary in different parts of the pool: longer periods in deep areas, shorter periods where it is shallow.

Disinfection and treatment will not remove all pollutants. The design of a swimming pool should recognize the need to dilute the pool water with fresh water. Dilution limits the buildup of pollutants from bathers (e.g. constituents of sweat and urine), the by-products of disinfection and various other dissolved chemicals and pollutants.

A drain must be installed at the lowest point in the pool, and drainage facilities need to be sufficient to ensure quick emptying. The drains from the pool should be independent; however, when they are connected to any other drainage system, a backwater valve must be installed in the recreational water environment to prevent cross-connections. Anti-vortex and anti-entanglement type drain covers must be provided, which are constructed of durable, easily visible and readily cleaned material.

Children's pools can have their own independent recirculation, filtration and halogenation system, because children are particularly potent sources of pathogens. The turnover rate of water needs to be sufficient, ideally higher than in adult pools, such as at least once every 30 minutes. Anti-vortex and anti-entanglement type drain covers must be provided that are constructed of durable, easily visible and readily cleaned material.

2. Bather load

A realistic bather load needs to be catered for during both design and operation of pools. The circulation and treatment systems and the hydraulic volume will determine the appropriate safe bather load, but the practicability of maintaining bather loads within design criteria also needs to be considered.

3. Filtration

Controlling clarity involves adequate water treatment, usually involving filtration and coagulation. Filtration is crucial to good water quality, affecting both aesthetic clarity and disinfection. Disinfection will be compromised by reduced clarity, as particles associated with turbidity can surround microorganisms and shield them from the action of disinfectants. In addition, filtration is important for removing *Cryptosporidium* oocysts and *Giardia* cysts and some other protozoa that are relatively resistant to chlorine disinfection.

Filters need to be designed to remove particles at a sufficient rate, such as removing all particles greater than 10 μm from the entire volume of the pool in 6 hours or less. Filters can be cartridge or media type (e.g. rapid-pressure sand filters, high-rate sand filters, diatomaceous earth filters or gravity sand filters). All media-type filters need to be capable of being backwashed. Filter accessories, such as pressure gauges, air-relief valves and rate-of-flow indicators, should be provided as required. Sufficient access to sand filters should be maintained so that they can be inspected at a regular frequency, at least on a weekly basis, and the media must be changed periodically.

Some of the factors that are important to consider in the design of a granular media (e.g. sand) filtration system include:

- *Filtration rate*: The higher the filtration rate, the lower the filtration efficiency. Some of the higher rate granular filters do not handle particles and colloids as effectively as medium-rate filters and cannot be used with coagulants.
- *Bed depth*: The correct sand bed depth is important for efficient filtration.
- *Number of filters*: Pools will benefit greatly from the increased flexibility and safeguards of having more than one filter. In particular, pools can remain in use with a reduced turnover on one filter while the other one is being inspected or repaired. Filtered water from one filter can be used to backwash another.

- *Backwashing*: The cleaning of a filter bed clogged with suspended solids is referred to as backwashing. It is accomplished by reversing the flow, fluidizing the sand and passing pool water back through the filters to waste. It should be initiated as recommended by the filter manufacturer, when the allowable turbidity value has been exceeded or when a certain length of time without backwashing has passed. The filter may take some time to settle once the flow is returned to normal, and water should not be returned to the pool until the filter has settled.

A hair strainer is required between the pool outlet and the suction side of the pumps to remove foreign debris such as hair, lint and pins. The removable portion of the strainer should be corrosion resistant and have holes that are smaller than 6 mm in diameter.

Coagulants (and flocculants) enhance the removal of dissolved, colloidal or suspended material by bringing this material out of solution or suspension as solids (coagulation), then clumping the solids together (flocculation), producing a floc, which is more easily trapped in the filter. Coagulants are particularly important in helping to remove the infective cysts of *Giardia* and oocysts of *Cryptosporidium* spp., which otherwise would pass through the filter. Coagulant efficiency is dependent on pH, which therefore needs to be controlled. Dosing pumps should be capable of accurately dosing the small quantities of coagulant required and adjusting to the requirements of the bather load. Coagulation is often required as a prerequisite to effective filtration, depending on the filtration process selected.

4. Chemical dosing, including disinfection

Disinfection is a process whereby pathogenic microorganisms are removed or inactivated by chemical (e.g. chlorination) or physical (e.g. filtration, UV radiation) means, such that they represent no significant risk of infection. Recirculating pool water is disinfected using the treatment process, and the entire water body is disinfected by application of a disinfectant residual, which inactivates agents added to the pool by bathers.

For disinfection to occur with any biocidal chemical, the oxidant demand of the water being treated must first be satisfied, and sufficient chemical must remain to effect disinfection.

Issues to be considered in the choice of a disinfectant and application system include:

- safety;
- comfort (e.g. avoiding skin irritation);

- compatibility with the source water (hardness and alkalinity);
- type and size of pool (disinfectant may be more readily degraded or lost through evaporation in outdoor pools);
- oxidation capacity;
- bather load (sweat and urine from bathers will increase disinfectant demand);
- operation of the pool (i.e. supervision and management).

The choice of disinfectant used as part of swimming-pool water treatment should ideally comply with the following criteria:

- effective, rapid inactivation of pathogenic microorganisms;
- capacity for ongoing oxidation to assist control of contaminants during pool use;
- a wide margin between effective biocidal concentration and the concentration resulting in adverse effects on human health;
- availability of a quick and easy determination of the disinfectant's concentration in pool water (simple analytical and test methods);
- potential to measure the disinfectant's concentration electrometrically to permit automatic control of disinfectant dosing and continuous recording of the values measured.

Commonly used disinfectants include the following:

- *Chlorine*: Chlorination is the most widely used pool water disinfectant, usually in the form of chlorine gas, sodium or calcium hypochlorite or chlorinated isocyanurates. Chlorine is inexpensive and relatively convenient to produce, store, transport and use. Chlorinated isocyanurate compounds, which are somewhat complex white crystalline compounds with slight chlorine-type odour that provide free chlorine when dissolved in water, are used in most small outdoor ship pools. They are an indirect source of chlorine, via an organic reserve (cyanuric acid). The relationship between the chlorine residual and the level of cyanuric acid is critical and can be difficult to maintain. Chlorinated isocyanurates are not suited to the variations in bather loads usually found in large pools. However, they are particularly useful in outdoor swimming pools exposed to direct sunlight, where UV radiation rapidly degrades free chlorine.
- *Ozone*: Ozone can be viewed as the most powerful oxidizing and disinfecting agent that is available for pool and spa water treatment. Ozone in combination with chlorine or bromine is a very effective disinfection system, but the use of ozone alone cannot ensure a residual disinfectant capacity throughout the swimming pool. Ozone

is most frequently used as a treatment step, followed by deozonation and addition of a residual disinfectant, such as chlorine. Excess ozone must be destroyed by an activated carbon filter, because this toxic gas could settle, to be breathed by pool users and staff. Residual disinfectants should also be removed by the activated carbon filter and are therefore added after this step.

- *UV radiation*: Like ozone, UV radiation is a plant-room treatment that purifies the circulating water, inactivating microorganisms and, to a certain extent, breaking down some pollutants by photo-oxidation. This decreases the chlorine demand of the purified water but does not leave a disinfectant residual in the pool water, so chlorine disinfection is still required. For UV to be most effective, the water must be pretreated to remove turbidity-causing particulate matter that prevents the penetration of the UV radiation or absorbs the UV energy.

Microbial colonization of surfaces can be a problem and is generally controlled through cleaning and disinfection, such as shock dosing.

The method of introducing disinfectants to the pool water influences their effectiveness. Individual disinfectants can have their own specific dosing requirements, but the following principles apply to all:

- Automatic dosing is preferable. Electronic sensors continuously monitor pH and residual disinfectant levels and adjust the dosing correspondingly to maintain correct levels. Regular verification of the system (including manual tests on pool water samples) and good management are important.
- Hand dosing (i.e. putting chemicals directly into the pool) is rarely justified. Manual systems of dosing must be backed up by good management of operation and monitoring. It is important that the pool remains empty of bathers until the chemical has dispersed.
- Trying to compensate for inadequacies in treatment by shock dosing is bad practice, because it can mask deficiencies in design or operation that may produce other problems and can generate unwelcome by-products.
- Dosing pumps should be designed to shut themselves off if the circulation system fails (although automatic dosing monitors should remain in operation) to ensure that chemical dispersion is interrupted.
- Residual disinfectants are generally dosed at the very end of the treatment process. The treatment methods of flocculation, filtration and ozonation serve to clarify the water, reduce the organic load

and greatly reduce the microbial count, so that the post-treatment disinfectant can be more effective and the amount of disinfectant that must be used can be minimized.

- It is important that disinfectants and pH-adjusting chemicals be well mixed with the water at the point of dosing.
- Dosing systems, like circulation, should continue 24 hours per day.

Production of disinfection by-products can be controlled by minimizing the introduction of their organic precursors (compounds that react with the disinfectant to yield the by-products) through good hygienic practices (pre-swim showering) and maximizing their removal by well-managed pool water treatment. Control of disinfection by-products involves dilution, treatment and disinfection modification or optimization. Because of the presence of bromide ions in salt water, a common by-product formed in the water and air of seawater pools on ships will be bromoform, which can result from either chlorine or ozone treatment.

It is inevitable that some volatile disinfection by-products will be produced in the pool water and escape into the air. This hazard can be managed to some extent through good ventilation.

The use of analysers helps to automate dosing and optimize conditions for pool safety, such as automatic dosing of chemicals for disinfection and pH adjustment. Water sample points must be provided throughout the system for testing halogen levels and routine calibration of the analyser. Analyser-controlled halogen-based disinfection equipment should be provided as required. It may be necessary to ensure that pH is adjusted by using appropriate acids and bases and that a buffering agent is used to stabilize the pH. This can be added to the functionality of the analyser.

5. *Legionella* control

In recreational water environments, it is impractical to maintain temperatures outside the range 25–50 °C. However, levels of *Legionella* spp. can be kept under control using appropriate management measures, including filtration and maintenance of a continuous disinfectant residual in recreational water environments and physical cleaning of all spa-pool equipment, including associated pipes and air-conditioning units. Rooms housing recreational water environments must be well ventilated to avoid an accumulation of *Legionella* spp. in the indoor air. Therefore, it is necessary to design and implement a range of other management strategies, which may include:

- adding biocides to the spa water, plumbing and filter. Whirlpool spas shall typically maintain a free chlorine residual between 3 and 10 mg/l or a free bromine residual between 4 and 10 mg/l (WHO, 2006). To ensure that free halogen is effective for disinfection, there is a need to maintain or regularly adjust the pH, typically in the range 7.2–7.8;
- ensuring that staff have appropriate training and skills to operate the recreational facility;
- applying a constant circulation of water in the whirlpool and spa pool;
- cleaning filter systems (e.g. by backwashing filters);
- cleaning pool surrounds;
- replacing a portion (e.g. 50%) of the water in each whirlpool and spa pool daily;
- completely draining whirlpools, spa pools and natural thermal pools and thoroughly physically cleaning all surfaces and all pipework regularly;
- maintaining and physically cleaning heating, ventilation and air-conditioning (HVAC) systems serving the room in which spa pools are located;
- installing signs that list standard safety precautions near the recreational water environments, which caution people who are immunocompromised or who are taking immunosuppressant medicines against using the recreational water environments.

Routine cleaning of the whole circulation system, including the spa, sprays, pumps and pipework, is critical and can require quite intensive doses of disinfectant, as *Legionella* spp. can persist in biofilms (scums on the surfaces of fittings and pipework), making them difficult to inactivate.

Bathers must be encouraged to shower before entering the water. This will remove pollutants such as perspiration, cosmetics and organic debris that can act as a source of nutrients for bacterial growth and as neutralizing agents for the oxidizing biocides. Bather density and duration in whirlpools and spa baths can also be controlled. Spa-pool facilities may require programmed rest periods during the day to allow recovery of disinfectant concentrations.

Testing for *Legionella* bacteria serves as a form of verification that the controls are working and should be undertaken periodically—for instance, monthly, quarterly or annually, depending on the type of ship environment. This testing should not replace or pre-empt the emphasis on control strategies. Furthermore, the tests are relatively specialized and need to be undertaken by properly equipped laboratories using experienced staff; they are therefore not generally performed by crews or during voyages. Verification sampling should focus on system extremities and high-risk sites.

6. Air quality

It is important to manage air quality as well as water quality in swimming pools, spas and similar recreational water environments. Rooms housing spas should be well ventilated to avoid an accumulation of *Legionella* spp. in the indoor air. In addition, ventilation will help reduce exposure to disinfection by-products in the air. Adequate ventilation should reduce risks from *Legionella* spp., but it is important that the system does not create its own risks. All surfaces of HVAC systems serving the room in which the spa or pool is located should be physically cleaned and disinfected to control biofilm.

Other design and construction aspects

The pool mechanical room must be readily accessible and well ventilated, and a potable water tap must be provided in this room. To help with ongoing maintenance, it is valuable to mark all piping with directional-flow arrows and maintain a flow diagram and operational instructions in a readily available location. The pool mechanical room and recirculation system need to be designed for easy and safe storage of chemicals and refilling of chemical feed tanks. Drains need to be installed in the pool mechanical room to allow for rapid draining of the entire pump and filter system, with a sufficiently large drain, at least 8 cm, being installed on the lowest point of the system.

To help reduce drowning risks, the depth of the pool and depth markers must be displayed prominently so that they can be seen from the deck and in the pool. Depth markers must be in either feet or metres, or both, and installed for every significant (1 m) change of depth.

B. Recirculating pools

The equipment and the operating procedures need to provide complete circulation of the water within the pool at a sufficient frequency, such as replacement of the water every 6 hours or less during pool operation. Equipment should include filters and other equipment and devices for disinfection and treatment that may be necessary to meet the requirements or recommendations of the national health administration of the country of registration. Self-priming, centrifugal pumps are suitable to recirculate pool water.

C. Flow-through pools

The flow-through swimming pool is probably the type most practicable for construction, installation and operation on board ships. The number of bathers that can use a swimming pool safely at one time and the total number that can use a pool during one day are governed by the area of the pool and the rate of replacement of its water. Therefore, the pool should be designed with special attention to the probable peak bather load and the maximum space available for the construction of a pool.

The following principles should be applied in the design of flow-through pools:

- The design capacity of the pool should be judged on the basis of the area, such as 2.6 m^2 per bather. For the maintenance of satisfactorily clean water in the pool, the rate of flow of clean water needs to be sufficient to achieve complete replacement every 6 hours or less. The water flowing through must be delivered to the pool through multiple inlets, located to ensure uniform distribution. These inlets can be served by a branch line taking off from the main supply line, at the pressure side of the filling valve near the pool. Control of the flow must be independent of the filling valve.
- The overflow must be discharged into skim gutters or a similar boundary overflow, with multiple outlets spaced not more than 3 m apart, and discharging to the waste system.
- The bottom of the pool should slope towards the drain or drains in such a manner as to effect complete drainage of the pool. In the interest of safety, the slope of any part of the pool bottom in which the water is less than a standing depth, 1.8 m deep, should not be more than a 1 in 15 gradient. For safety, there should be no sudden change of slope within the area where the water depth is shallow, less than 1.5 m.
- To help reduce drowning risks, the depth of the pool and depth markers must be displayed prominently so that they can be seen from the deck and in the pool. Depth markers must be in either feet or metres, or both, and installed for every significant (1 m) change of depth.

It is preferable to have a separate water supply system, including the pump, for recreational water environments. The water intake must be forward of all sewage and drainage outlets. However, if the pool is to be filled and operated only when the ship is under way, the fire or sanitary water pumps, or a combination of these pumps, may be used, noting that the following can be used to reduce contamination risks:

- The delivery line to the pool should be independent of other lines originating at or near the discharge of the pump or the valve manifold or at a point where the maximum or near-maximum flushing of the fire or sanitary water pump is routinely effected.
- If seawater is drawn into the pool, water should not be drawn when the ship is in port or, if under way, in contaminated waters. A readily accessible shut-off valve should be located close to the point from which the water is drawn and labelled "CLOSE WHILE IN HARBOURS".

Flow-through seawater supply systems for pools shall be used only while the ship is under way and at sea beyond 12 nautical miles from land. The pool (when in flow-through seawater mode) should be drained before the ship reaches port and should remain empty while in port. If the pool is not drained before arriving in port, the pool's seawater filling system should be shut off 12 nautical miles before reaching land, and a recirculation system should be used with appropriate filtering and halogenation.

D. Whirlpool spas

Whirlpools are subject to high bather loads relative to the volume of water. With high water temperatures and rapid agitation of water, it may become difficult to maintain satisfactory pH, microbiological quality and disinfectant residuals; therefore, additional care must be taken in the operation of whirlpools.

Potable water supplied to whirlpool systems must be supplied through an air gap or approved backflow preventer. Water filtration equipment needs to be able to remove all particles greater than 10 μm from the entire whirlpool water volume in 30 minutes or less. Filters can be cartridge filters, rapid-pressure sand filters, high-rate sand filters, diatomaceous earth filters or gravity sand filters. A clear sight glass can be added on the backwash side of the filters.

The overflow system must be designed so that the water level is maintained. It is advisable that whirlpool overflows be either directed by gravity to the make-up tank for recirculation through the filter system or disposed of as waste. Self-priming, centrifugal pumps must be used to recirculate whirlpool water.

Sufficient skimmers, one for every 14 m^2 or fraction thereof of water surface area, should be provided. The fill level of the whirlpool needs to be at the skim gutter level to enable skimming to take effect.

A temperature-control mechanism is required to prevent the temperature from exceeding 40 °C to avoid scalding and overheating.

A make-up tank may be used to replace water lost by splashing and evaporation. An overflow line at least twice the diameter of the supply line and located below the tank supply line should be used.

The system needs to permit regular (e.g. daily) shock treatment or superhalogenation. Halogenation equipment that is capable of maintaining the appropriate levels of free halogen throughout the use period must be included.

E. Spa pools

Spa pools have different operating conditions and present a special set of problems to operators. The design and operation of these facilities make it difficult to achieve adequate disinfectant residuals. They may require higher disinfectant residuals because of higher bather loads and temperatures, both of which lead to more rapid loss of a disinfectant residual.

A *Pseudomonas aeruginosa* concentration of less than 1 cfu/100 ml should be readily achievable through good management practices. Risk management measures that can be taken to deal with these non-enteric bacteria include ventilation, cleaning of equipment and verifying the adequacy of disinfection.

Spa pools that do not use disinfection require alternative methods of water treatment to keep the water microbiologically safe. A very high rate of water exchange is necessary—even if not fully effective—if there is no other way of preventing microbial contamination.

In spa pools where the use of disinfectants is undesirable or where it is difficult to maintain an adequate disinfectant residual, superheating spa water to 70 °C on a daily basis during periods of non-use may help control microbial proliferation.

To prevent overloading of spa pools, some countries recommend that clearly identifiable seats be installed for users combined with a minimum pool volume being defined for every seat, a minimum total pool volume and a maximum water depth.

4.2.2 Guideline 4.2: Pool hygiene

Guideline 4.2—Pool hygiene is continuously maintained.

Indicators for Guideline 4.2

1. Pre-swim showering is promoted.
2. Pre-swim use of toilets is promoted.
3. Effective procedures are in place to respond to vomitus and AFRs.

Guidance notes for Guideline 4.2

1. Pre-swim showering

Pre-swim showers will remove traces of sweat, urine, faecal matter, cosmetics, suntan oil and other potential water contaminants. The result will be cleaner pool water, easier disinfection using a smaller amount of chemicals and water that is more pleasant to swim in.

Pre-swim showers should be located adjacent to the swimming pool and be provided with water of drinking-water quality, as children and some adults may ingest the shower water. Shower water must run to waste.

2. Visiting toilets pre-swim

Toilets must be provided where they can be conveniently used before entering the pool and after leaving the pool. Users should be encouraged to use the toilets before bathing to minimize urination in the pool and AFRs. Parents need to encourage children to empty their bladders before they swim. Children below a certain age, such as below two years old, may not be permitted to use some pools.

3. Vomitus and accidental faecal releases

It is necessary to minimize AFRs and vomitus and to respond effectively to them when they occur. AFRs appear to occur relatively frequently, and it is likely that most go undetected. A pool operator faced with an AFR or vomitus in the pool water needs to act immediately.

If a faecal release is a solid stool, it can simply be retrieved quickly and discarded appropriately. The scoop used to retrieve it must be disinfected so that any bacteria and viruses adhering to it are inactivated and will not be returned to the pool the next time the scoop is used. As long as the pool is in other respects operating properly (disinfecting residuals, etc.), no further action is necessary.

If the stool is runny (diarrhoea) or if there is vomitus, the situation is potentially hazardous. Even though most disinfectants deal relatively well with many bacterial and viral agents in AFRs and vomitus, the possibility exists that the diarrhoea or vomitus is from someone infected with one of the protozoan parasites, *Cryptosporidium* and *Giardia*. The infectious stages (oocysts/cysts) are relatively resistant to chlorine disinfectants in the concentrations that are practical to use. The pool must therefore be cleared of bathers immediately.

The safest action, if the incident has occurred in a small pool, hot tub or whirlpool, is to empty and clean it before refilling and reopening. However, this may not be possible in larger pools.

If draining down is not possible, then the procedure given below—an imperfect solution that will only reduce, but not remove, risk—can be followed:

- The pool is cleared of people immediately.
- Disinfectant levels are maintained at the top of the recommended range.
- The pool is vacuumed and swept.
- Using a coagulant, the water is filtered for six turnover cycles. This could take up to a day and so might mean closing the pool until the next day.
- The filter is backwashed (and the water run to waste).
- The pool is reopened.

There are a few practical actions that pool operators can take to help prevent faecal release into the pools:

- No child (or adult) with a recent history of diarrhoea should swim.
- Parents should be encouraged to make sure that their children use the toilet before they swim.
- Thorough pre-swim showering is a good idea, and parents should encourage their children to do it.
- Young children should, whenever possible, be confined to pools small enough to drain in the event of an accidental release of faeces or vomitus.
- Lifeguards or pool attendants, if present, should be made responsible for looking out for and acting on AFR or vomitus.

4.2.3 Guideline 4.3: Monitoring

Guideline 4.3—Key parameters are monitored and maintained within target ranges.

Indicators for Guideline 4.3

1. Pool water turbidity is maintained within target ranges.
2. Disinfectant levels and pH are maintained within target ranges.
3. Microbial quality is maintained within target ranges, and there are effective procedures in place to respond to adverse detection events.

Guidance notes for Guideline 4.3

Frequent monitoring of control measures will help to provide early warning of deviations and could include:

- checking and adjusting the disinfectant residual and pH;
- inspection of maintenance and cleaning operations;
- inspection of the physical condition of recreational water environments, filters and equipment;
- undertaking surveillance for lower respiratory illness (e.g. pneumonia) among passengers and staff by recording all visits to the ship's medical office for confirmed or suspected pneumonia.

Parameters that are easy and inexpensive to measure and of immediate health relevance—that is, turbidity, disinfectant residual and pH—must be monitored frequently and in all pool types.

1. Turbidity

The ability to see either a small child at the bottom of the pool or markings on the pool bottom from the lifeguard's or pool attendant's position while the water surface is in movement is important. A turbidity limit of 0.5 nephelometric turbidity unit (NTU), or equivalent measurement, provides a good target value for well-treated water. Exceedance of turbidity limits suggests both a significant deterioration in water quality and a significant health hazard. Such exceedance merits immediate investigation and may lead to closure of the facility pending remedial action.

2. Disinfectant levels and pH

For a conventional public swimming pool with good hydraulics and filtration, operating within its design bather load, adequate routine disinfection should be achieved with a free chlorine level of 1 mg/l throughout the pool. In a well-operated pool, it is possible to achieve such a residual with maximum levels at any single point below 2 mg/l for pools. Lower residuals (0.5 mg/l) will be acceptable in combination with the additional use of ozone or UV disinfection, whereas higher levels (ranging from 2 to 3 mg/l) may be required for hot tubs, because of higher bather loads and higher temperatures (WHO, 2006).

Disinfectant residuals must be checked by sampling the pool before it opens and during the opening period (ideally, during a period of high bather load) (WHO, 2006). The frequency of testing during swimming-pool use depends on the nature and use of the swimming pool. Samples should be taken at a depth of 5–30 cm. It is good practice to include as a routine sampling point the area of the pool where the disinfectant residual is lowest. Occasional samples should be taken from other parts of the pool and circulation system. If the routine test results are outside the recommended ranges, the situation needs to be assessed and action taken.

The pH value of swimming-pool water needs to be maintained within the recommended range to ensure optimal disinfection and coagulation. The pH should be maintained between 7.2 and 7.8 for chlorine disinfectants and between 7.2 and 8.0 for bromine-based and other non-chlorine disinfection processes (WHO, 2006). In order to do so, regular pH measurements are essential, and either continuous or intermittent adjustment is usually necessary. For heavily used pools, the pH value must be measured continuously and adjusted automatically. For less frequently used pools, it may be sufficient to measure the pH manually.

To avoid the formation of excessive disinfection by-products or irritation of mucosal surfaces by disinfectants, disinfectant residuals should be maintained at levels that are consistent with satisfactory microbiological quality but that are not unnecessarily excessive. Operators should attempt to maintain free chlorine residual levels below 5 mg/l at all points in the pool or spa.

3. Microbial quality

There is limited risk of significant microbial contamination and illness in a well-managed pool or similar environment with an adequate residual disinfectant concentration, a pH value maintained at an appropriate level, well-operated filters and frequent monitoring of non-microbial parameters. Nevertheless, samples of pool water from public pools should be monitored at appropriate intervals for microbial parameters, including HPC, thermotolerant coliforms or *E. coli*, *Pseudomonas aeruginosa*, *Legionella* spp. and *Staphylococcus aureus*. The frequency of monitoring and the guideline values vary according to microbial parameter and the type of pool.

Where operational guidelines are exceeded, pool operators should check turbidity, residual disinfectant levels and pH and then resample. When critical guidelines are exceeded, the pool should be closed while investigation and remediation are conducted.

The following monitoring of microbial quality is recommended:

- The HPC (37 °C for 24 hours) gives an indication of the overall bacterial population within the pool. It is recommended that operational levels should be less than 200 cfu/ml.
- Thermotolerant coliforms and *E. coli* are indicators of faecal contamination. Either thermotolerant coliforms or *E. coli* should be measured in pools, hot tubs and spas. Operational levels should be less than 1 cfu or 1 most probable number (mpn) per 100 ml.
- Routine monitoring of *Pseudomonas aeruginosa* is recommended in hot tubs and spas. It is suggested for swimming pools when there is evidence of operational problems (e.g. failure of disinfection or problems relating to filters or water pipes), a deterioration in the quality of the pool water or known health problems. It is recommended that, for continuously disinfected pools, operational levels should be below 1 cfu/100 ml. If high counts are found (>100 cfu/100 ml), pool operators should check turbidity, disinfectant residuals and pH, resample, backwash thoroughly, wait one turnover and resample. If high levels of *P. aeruginosa* remain, the pool should be closed, and a thorough cleaning and disinfection programme should be initiated. Hot tubs should be shut down, drained, cleaned and refilled.
- Periodic testing for *Legionella* spp. is useful, especially for hot tubs, in order to determine whether filters are being colonized. It is recommended that operational levels should be below 1 cfu/100 ml. Where this is exceeded, hot tubs should be shut down, drained, cleaned and refilled. Shock chlorination may be appropriate if it is suspected that filters have become colonized.
- Routine monitoring of *Staphylococcus aureus* is not recommended, although monitoring may be undertaken as part of a wider investigation into the quality of the water when health problems associated with the pool are suspected. Where samples are taken, levels should be less than 100 cfu/100 ml.

Further advice on testing for *Legionella* spp. can be found in Bartram et al. (2007).

5 Ballast water

5.1 Background

This chapter deals with the management of ballast water, including its storage and safe disposal.

5.1.1 Health risks associated with ballast water on ships

Many ships use water as ballast to maintain stability and navigate safely, carrying from 30% to 50% of the total cargo in ballast water. This represents a volume that varies from a few hundred litres up to more than 10 million litres per ship. Therefore, this water presents an important risk to human health, with the possibility of introducing new endemic diseases and spreading disease by transferring pathogens and harmful organisms. In this context, more than 7000 marine species travel daily, and approximately 10 billion tonnes of ballast water are transported annually by ship. Concern regarding transfer of ballast water and sediments from ships has increased, and there is a theoretical possibility of transporting hazards such as toxigenic *Vibrio cholerae* O1 and O139, which might then be associated with cholera outbreaks in port areas.

5.1.2 Standards

The Marine Environment Protection Committee has adopted, since 1993, voluntary guidelines for the prevention of risks from unwanted organisms through ballast water and sediments from ships. In 1997, the IMO Assembly adopted, through Resolution A.868(20), the Guidelines for the Control and Management of Ships' Ballast Water to Minimize the Transfer of Harmful Aquatic Organisms and Pathogens (IMO, 1998).

The IMO International Convention for the Control and Management of Ships' Ballast Water and Sediments[1] was adopted in February 2004. The objective of this convention is to prevent, minimize and ultimately eliminate risks to the environment, human health, property and resources arising from the transfer of harmful aquatic organisms and pathogens through the control and management of ships' ballast water and sediments; to provide guidance to avoid unwanted side-effects from the control measures put in place; and to encourage development

1 http://www.imo.org/About/Conventions/ListOfConventions/Pages/International-Convention-for-the-Control-and-Management-of-Ships'-Ballast-Water-and-Sediments-(BWM).aspx (accessed 30 January 2011).

in related knowledge and technology. The measures for inspection and control of the sanitary risks of ballast water tank sediments must consider the procedures established in the IMO International Convention for the Control and Management of Ships' Ballast Water and Sediments. From 2009, but not later than 2016, the convention requires the establishment of a ballast water management system on board ships, which will replace the uncontrolled ballast water uptake and discharge operations common until then. In future, ballast water will have to be treated on board before being discharged into the marine environment, in compliance with the Ballast Water Performance Standard in Regulation D-2 of the convention.

Parties to the convention are given the right to take, individually or jointly with other Parties, more stringent measures with respect to the prevention, reduction or elimination of the transfer of harmful aquatic organisms and pathogens through the control and management of ships' ballast water and sediments, consistent with international law.

5.2 Guidelines

This section provides user-targeted information and guidance, identifying responsibilities and providing examples of practices that can control risks. Two specific *guidelines* (situations to aim for and maintain) are presented, each of which is accompanied by a set of *indicators* (measures for whether the guidelines are met) and *guidance notes* (advice on applying the guidelines and indicators in practice, highlighting the most important aspects that need to be considered when setting priorities for action).

In some cases, ballast water treatment systems have failed to perform as required, resulting in unsafe situations. Therefore, reliance should not be placed on treatment and management systems alone. Multiple ballast management barriers should be actively maintained, including:

- filling with ballast water from safe environments wherever practicable;
- matching ballast treatment facilities to their required capacities;
- maintaining sound practices in discharging ballast water.

Staff at ports and ship crews need to be adequately trained in the protection of the environment, safe operation (including collection, handling and disposal of wastes) and relevant legislation.

5.2.1 Guideline 5.1: Ballast water management

Guideline 5.1—A ballast water management plan is designed and implemented.

Indicators for Guideline 5.1

1. An approved ballast water management plan is in place and reviewed regularly.
2. Ballast water management requirements and practices are carried out as per the approved plan.
3. A ballast water record book is kept, with accurate records maintained.
4. Audit measures are in place and adhered to.

Guidance notes for Guideline 5.1

Ships are required to implement a ballast water management plan approved by the administration (Regulation B-1 of the IMO International Convention for the Control and Management of Ships' Ballast Water and Sediments). The ballast water management plan is specific to each ship and includes a detailed description of the actions to be taken to implement the ballast water management requirements and supplemental ballast water management practices.

Ballast water management systems must be approved by the administration in accordance with IMO guidelines for the approval of ballast water management systems (Resolution MEPC.174(58)). These include systems that make use of chemicals or biocides, make use of organisms or biological mechanisms, or alter the chemical or physical characteristics of the ballast water.

Ships must have a ballast water record book (Regulation B-2) to record when ballast water is taken on board, circulated or treated for ballast water management purposes and discharged into the sea. It should also record when ballast water is discharged to a reception facility and accidental or other exceptional discharges of ballast water.

Ships are required to be surveyed and certified (Article 7—Survey and Certification) and may be inspected by port State control officers (Article 9—Inspection of Ships) who can verify that the ship has a valid certificate, inspect the ballast water record book and/or sample the ballast water. If there are concerns, a detailed inspection may be carried out, and "the Party carrying out the inspection shall take such steps as will ensure that the ship shall not discharge Ballast Water until it can do so without presenting a threat of harm to the environment, human health, property or resources".

The specific requirements for ballast water management are contained in Regulation B-3—Ballast Water Management for Ships:

- Ships constructed before 2009 with a ballast water capacity of between 1500 and 5000 cubic metres must conduct ballast water management that at least meets the ballast water exchange standards or the ballast water performance standards until 2014, after which time it shall at least meet the ballast water performance standard.
- Ships constructed before 2009 with a ballast water capacity of less than 1500 or greater than 5000 cubic metres must conduct ballast water management that at least meets the ballast water exchange standards or the ballast water performance standards until 2016, after which time it shall at least meet the ballast water performance standard.
- Ships constructed in or after 2009 with a ballast water capacity of less than 5000 cubic metres must conduct ballast water management that at least meets the ballast water performance standard.
- Ships constructed in or after 2009 but before 2012, with a ballast water capacity of 5000 cubic metres or more shall conduct ballast water management that at least meets the standard described in regulation D-1 or D-2 until 2016 and at least the ballast water performance standard after 2016.
- Ships constructed in or after 2012, with a ballast water capacity of 5000 cubic metres or more shall conduct ballast water management that at least meets the ballast water performance standard.

5.2.2 Guideline 5.2: Ballast water treatment and disposal

Guideline 5.2—Ballast water is safely treated and disposed of.

Indicators for Guideline 5.2

1. Disposal of ballast water is carried out safely.
2. Overboard discharge of ballast water is carried out only within permitted bounds.

Guidance notes for Guideline 5.2

1. Disposal of ballast water

Ships are not generally permitted to discharge ballast water, bilge water or any other liquid containing contaminating or toxic wastes within an area from which water for a water supply is drawn or in any area restricted from the discharge of wastes by any national or local authority. Overboard discharge in harbours, ports and coastal waters is subject to the regulations of the governing authorities in these areas. Sewage, food particles, putrescible matter and toxic substances must not be discharged to the bilge.

The IMO International Convention for the Control and Management of Ships' Ballast Water and Sediments has defined a ballast water exchange standard and a ballast water performance standard.

As per Regulation D-1—Ballast Water Exchange Standard, ships performing ballast water exchange shall do so with an efficiency of 95% volumetric exchange. For ships exchanging ballast water by the pumping-through method, pumping through three times the volume of each ballast water tank shall be considered to meet the standard described. Pumping through less than three times the volume may be accepted, provided that the ship can demonstrate that at least 95% volumetric exchange is met.

As per Regulation D-2—Ballast Water Performance Standard, ships conducting ballast water management shall discharge fewer than 10 viable organisms per cubic metre greater than or equal to 50 μm in minimum dimension and fewer than 10 viable organisms per millilitre less than 50 μm in minimum dimension and greater than or equal to 10 μm in minimum dimension; and discharge of the indicator microbes shall not exceed the specified concentrations.

The indicator microbes, as a human health standard, include, but are not limited to:

- toxicogenic *Vibrio cholerae* (O1 and O139): less than 1 cfu/100 ml or less than 1 cfu/g wet weight zooplankton samples;
- *Escherichia coli*: less than 250 cfu/100 ml;
- intestinal enterococci: less than 100 cfu/100 ml.

Other methods of ballast water management may also be accepted as alternatives to the ballast water exchange standard and ballast water performance standard, provided that such methods ensure at least the same level of protection of the environment, human health, property or resources and are approved in principle by the IMO's Marine Environment Protection Committee.

Under Article 5—Sediment Reception Facilities, Parties undertake to ensure that ports and terminals where cleaning or repair of ballast tanks occurs have adequate reception facilities for the intake of sediments. Barges and/or trucks for the reception of liquid wastes or shore connections at ports to receive these wastes into a sewer system are typically provided at ports. Where the port servicing area or barge does not provide a hose and suitable connections to receive liquid wastes, a ship must provide a special hose and connections large enough to allow rapid discharge of the wastes to sewer or other suitable point. This hose needs to be durable and impervious and have a smooth interior surface. It must be of a fitting different from that of the potable water hose or other water-filling hose, and it must be labelled "FOR WASTE DISCHARGE ONLY". After use, the hose must be cleaned, disinfected and stored in a convenient place labelled "WASTE DISCHARGE HOSE".

2. Overboard discharge of ballast water

Under Regulation B-4—Ballast Water Exchange of the IMO International Convention for the Control and Management of Ships' Ballast Water and Sediments, all ships using ballast water exchange should:

- whenever possible, conduct ballast water exchange at least 200 nautical miles from the nearest land and in water at least 200 metres in depth, taking into account Guidelines developed by IMO;
- in cases where the ship is unable to conduct ballast water exchange as above, this should be as far from the nearest land as possible, and in all cases at least 50 nautical miles from the nearest land and in water at least 200 metres in depth.

When these requirements cannot be met, areas where ships can conduct ballast water exchange may be designated. All ships shall remove and dispose of sediments from spaces designated to carry ballast water in accordance with the provisions of the ships' ballast water management plan (Regulation B-4).

6 Waste management and disposal

6.1 Background

This chapter deals with the management of solid waste (e.g. garbage) and liquid waste (e.g. sewage and greywater) on board ship, including their storage and safe disposal.

6.1.1 Health risks associated with wastes on ships

Unsafe management and disposal of ship wastes can readily lead to adverse health consequences. Humans can become exposed directly, both on ship and at port, as a result of contact with waste that is not being managed in a safe manner. Exposure can also occur via the environmental transfer of disease-causing organisms or harmful substances due to unsafe disposal. However, waste can be managed and disposed of in ways that prevent harm from occurring.

Waste can contain hazardous microbial, chemical or physical agents. For example, sharp objects are in themselves dangerous and may harbour infectious agents. Used syringes are a good example and can transmit disease-causing agents, such as hepatitis C virus and human immunodeficiency virus.

Risks of harm arising as a result of improperly managed ship waste are increasing with the greater number of ships in service and the increase in habitation in port areas. Waste streams on ships include sewage, greywater and garbage, as well as effluent from oil/water separators, cooling water, boiler and steam generator blow-down, medical wastes (e.g. health-care wastes, laboratory wastes and veterinary-care wastes), industrial wastewater (e.g. from photo processing) and hazardous waste (radioactive, chemical and biological wastes and unwanted pharmaceuticals).

Food wastes and refuse readily attract rodents, flies and cockroaches, for example, which are reservoirs and vectors of etiological agents of many diseases (see chapter 7).

Restrictions on depositing hazardous wastes into water bodies mean that ships need to capture and retain those wastes on board for periods of time. The process of packaging and storing hazardous wastes is in itself hazardous to the crew, and the storage of hazardous wastes leads to the risk of harm arising should spills or leaks occur. Waste needs to be appropriately disposed of in accordance with the rules and regulations applicable at the point of disposal.

6.1.2 Standards

Waste management from ships is covered in the IHR 2005 and in more detail in the International Convention for the Prevention of Pollution from Ships (MARPOL 73/78, as amended).[1] MARPOL was adopted by the International Conference on Marine Pollution in 1973 and has been subject to numerous amendments as it is updated, including the 1978 protocol and amendments collated into a consolidated version in 2002. Regulations covering the various sources of ship-generated pollution are contained in the six annexes of the Convention:

- Annex I. Regulations for the Prevention of Pollution by Oil;
- Annex II. Regulations for the Control of Pollution by Noxious Liquid Substances in Bulk;
- Annex III. Prevention of Pollution by Harmful Substances Carried by Sea in Packaged Form;
- Annex IV. Prevention of Pollution by Sewage from Ships (date of entry into force, 27 September 2003);
- Annex V. Prevention of Pollution by Garbage from Ships;
- Annex VI. Prevention of Air Pollution from Ships (adopted September 1997).

Medical waste requires special management. Specifically, details of health-care waste management can be found at http://www.healthcarewaste.org/en/115_overview.html and in the *Guidelines for safe disposal of unwanted pharmaceuticals in and after emergencies* (WHO, 1999).

6.2 Guidelines

This section provides user-targeted information and guidance, identifying responsibilities and providing examples of practices that can control risks. Three specific *guidelines* (situations to aim for and maintain) are presented, each of which is accompanied by a set of *indicators* (measures for whether the guidelines are met) and *guidance notes* (advice on applying the guidelines and indicators in practice, highlighting the most important aspects that need to be considered when setting priorities for action).

Outbreaks and harm associated with waste have been linked to poor storage and disposal practices. Once generated, stored waste becomes a potential source of harm. Therefore, the first disease prevention strategy should be to minimize the amount of hazardous waste generated as far as

[1] http://www.imo.org/About/Conventions/ListOfConventions/Pages/International-Convention-for-the-Prevention-of-Pollution-from-Ships-(MARPOL).aspx (accessed 30 January 2011).

practicable. It is also necessary to ensure that the systems for collecting and storing waste are adequate given the extent and nature of waste generated on board ship.

In some cases, waste-management treatment systems have failed to perform as required, resulting in unsafe situations. Therefore, reliance should not be placed on treatment and management systems alone. Multiple waste-management barriers should be actively maintained, including:

- considering how waste is generated on board, and choosing activities and practices that produce the least hazardous waste in the first place;
- matching waste-management treatment facilities to their required capacities;
- maintaining sound practices in collecting and storing waste.

Staff at ports and ship crews need to be adequately trained in the protection of the environment, safe operation and relevant legislation. People involved in the collection, handling and disposal of wastes need to be trained in the relevant legislation and the risks posed by wastes.

6.2.1 Guideline 6.1: Sewage and greywater management

Guideline 6.1—Sewage and greywater are safely treated and disposed of.

Indicators for Guideline 6.1

1. The sanitary system adequately contains the liquid waste, and sewage and greywater are disposed of safely within permitted bounds.
2. Grease traps are used to manage greasy liquid wastes.
3. Appropriate treatment is applied, where required, before storage or discharge of sewage and greywater.

Guidance notes for Guideline 6.1

1. Disposal of sewage and liquid wastes

Ships are not generally permitted to discharge sewage or any other liquid containing contaminating or toxic wastes within an area from which a water supply is drawn or in any area restricted for the discharge of wastes by any national or local authority. Overboard discharge in harbours, ports and coastal waters is subject to the regulations of the governing authorities in these areas. Sewage, food particles, putrescible matter and toxic substances must not be discharged to the bilge.

Any country may provide special barges for the receipt of these wastes or shore connections that input to the sewer system. Where the shore servicing area or barge does not provide a hose or connections to receive these wastes, the ship must provide a special hose and connections large enough to allow rapid discharge of wastes. This hose must be durable and impervious, have a smooth interior surface, be of a size different from that of the potable water hose or other water-filling hoses and be labelled "FOR WASTE DISCHARGE ONLY". After use, the hose must be cleaned by thorough flushing with clear water and stored in a convenient place labelled "WASTE DISCHARGE HOSE".

The prohibition against discharge of wastes near a water supply intake or in any body of water where measures for the prevention and control of pollution are in force will require the provision of retention tanks or sewage-treatment equipment on board.

Systems need to be designed and constructed so as not to leak wastes and need to be amenable to ready inspection to check for leaks or bursts. Approved backflow preventers (vacuum breakers) or acceptable air gaps must be installed in the water supply lines to the grinders. All piping should be colour coded and labelled (e.g. according to ISO 14726:2006) at least every 5 m to avoid confusion and possible cross-connection to potable water. Drain, soil and waste pipes need to be maintained frequently to prevent clogging and the backflow of sewage, greywater or contaminated wastes into the fixtures and spaces served by the collection system.

2. Grease traps

All galley wastes, exclusive of ground refuse, that may contain grease must be made to flow through grease interceptors (grease traps) to a retaining box before discharge or treatment on board ship. The design of the interceptors may need to be approved by the appropriate authority of the country of registration. The grease collected may be disposed of by incineration, by storage for shore disposal or by overboard discharge on the high seas. Overboard discharge may occur after a suitable separation distance with the closest line of land, such as 3 nautical miles (12 nautical miles in territorial sea), in compliance with other national rules.

3. Treatment

All ships must be equipped with facilities for managing wastes from toilets and urinals, hospital facilities and medical-care areas, and food refuse grinders. These facilities include treatment systems and/or safe holding tanks, properly equipped with pumps and piping. Wastes from safe holding tanks may be discharged to port connections or to special barges or trucks. The design of treatment systems and waste-holding tanks needs to be based on a suitable volume (e.g. 114 litres of liquid waste per capita per day) and may need to be approved by the appropriate authority of the country of registration.

For ships where the normal wastewater flow to be treated is quite large, exceeding 4750 litres per day, treatment must be designed to produce effluent of a suitable quality, such as biochemical oxygen demand of 50 mg/l or less, a suspended solids content of 150 mg/l or less and a coliform count of 1000 or less per 100 ml.

Excess sludge must be stored for appropriate disposal to land-based facilities or when on the high seas. For ships with a daily flow of wastewater to be treated that is quite small, less than 4750 litres, treatment may be limited to passing the wastes through grinders, followed by disinfection to produce an effluent with a coliform count of 1000 or less per 100 ml.

Chlorination, or an equally effective method of disinfection, may need to be installed, as recommended by the manufacturer, to produce an effluent meeting the coliform requirements set by the relevant authorities.

6.2.2 Guideline 6.2: Solid waste management

Guideline 6.2—Solid waste is safely treated and disposed of.

Indicators for Guideline 6.2

1. Garbage is safely stored in appropriately designed facilities.
2. Excess sludge is stored safely prior to appropriate disposal.

Guidance notes for Guideline 6.2

1. Facilities for waste storage

To prevent corrosion, the interiors of food and garbage lifts may need to be constructed of stainless steel and meet the same standards required for the storage, preparation and service of food. Decks need to be constructed of a durable, non-absorbent, non-corroding material and have a suitable internal cove, at least 10 mm along all sides. Bulkhead-mounted air vents must be positioned in the upper portion of the panels or in the deckhead. To help with cleaning and removal of spills, a drain at the bottom of all lift shafts must be provided, including the provision of platform lifts and dumbwaiters.

If used to transport waste, the interiors of dumbwaiters must be readily cleanable and constructed of stainless steel or similar and meet the same standards as other food service areas. The bottom of the dumbwaiter should include a suitable cover.

Garbage chutes, if installed, need to be constructed of stainless steel or similar and have an automatic cleaning system.

In waste-management equipment wash rooms, bulkheads, deckheads and decks need to be constructed to meet the same standards required for the storage, preparation and service of food. A bulkhead-mounted pressure washing system could be provided with a deck sink and drain. An enclosed automatic equipment washing machine or room may be used in place of the pressure washing system and deck sink. Adequate ventilation is required for extraction of steam and heat.

The garbage storage room should be well ventilated, and the temperature and humidity controlled. A sealed, refrigerated space must be used for storing wet garbage. The space needs to meet the same criteria for cold storage facilities for food. The room must be of adequate size to hold unprocessed waste for the longest expected period when off-loading of waste is not possible and must be separated from all food preparation and storage areas.

In all the garbage holding and processing facilities, there need to be easily accessible hand-washing stations with potable hot and cold water, hose connections and a sufficient number of deck drains to prevent any pooling of water. The sorting tables in garbage processing areas must be constructed from stainless steel or similar and have coved corners and rounded edges. Deck coaming, if provided, needs to be adequate, at least 8 cm, and coved. If the tables have drains, they should be directed to the deck drain, which requires a strainer. A storage locker must be provided for cleaning materials to keep them away from foods. Adequate lighting, at least 220 lux, is required at work-surface levels, and light fixtures need to be recessed or fitted with stainless-steel or similar guards to prevent breakage.

To facilitate storage, tops and bottoms must be removed from all empty metal containers or containers with metal ends, and the remaining parts flattened. Containers of paper, wood, plastic and similar materials should also be flattened for convenient space-saving storage. Dry refuse must be stored in tightly covered bins or in closed compartments, protected against weather, wash and the entry of rodents and vermin. The containers must be thoroughly cleaned after emptying and treated with insecticides or pesticides, if necessary, to discourage harbourage of rodents and vermin.

2. Excess sludge

Excess sludge is typically stored appropriately for appropriate disposal to land-based facilities or when on the high seas.

6.2.3 Guideline 6.3: Health-care and pharmaceutical waste management

Guideline 6.3—Health-care and pharmaceutical waste is safely treated and disposed of.

Indicator for Guideline 6.3

1. Health-care and pharmaceutical waste is safely treated and disposed of.

Guidance notes for Guideline 6.3

Pharmaceutical wastes produced on board must be managed appropriately in order to prevent harm to the environment and human health. Specific considerations for pharmaceutical wastes include avoiding disposal of non-biodegradable products or products that might harm bacteria involved in wastewater treatment into the sewage system and avoiding burning pharmaceuticals at low temperatures or in open containers.

Health-care waste is any waste generated during patient diagnosis, treatment or immunization. Health-care waste is of two categories: infectious and non-infectious. Infectious health-care waste is liquid or solid waste that contains pathogens in sufficient numbers and with sufficient virulence to cause infectious disease in susceptible hosts exposed to the waste. Non-infectious health-care waste includes disposable health-care supplies and materials that do not fall into the category of infectious health-care waste.

All ships should be equipped with facilities for treating and/or safely storing health-care wastes. Infectious waste must be safely stored or sterilized (e.g. by steam) and suitably packaged for ultimate disposal ashore. Health-care waste should be clearly labelled. Ships properly equipped may incinerate paper- and cloth-based health-care waste, but not plastic and wet materials. Sharps must be collected in plastic autoclavable sharps containers and retained on board for ultimate disposal ashore. Unused sharps must be disposed of ashore in the same manner as health-care waste.

Liquid health-care wastes may be disposed of by discharging them into the sewage system. Non-infectious health-care waste may be disposed of as garbage if it does not require steam sterilizing or special handling. Staff dealing with health-care wastes must be immunized against hepatitis B virus.

Note the WHO *International medical guide for ships* (WHO, 2007), and note that some country medical guides are also available.

7 Vector and reservoir control

7.1 Background

This chapter deals with the management of disease vectors and their reservoirs on board ship.

The IHR 2005 state that conveyance operators should "permanently keep conveyances for which they are responsible free of sources of infection or contamination, including vectors and reservoirs". Every conveyance leaving an area where vector control is recommended by WHO should be disinfected and kept free from vectors. When there are methods and materials recommended by WHO, these should be employed. States should accept disinfection, deratting and other control measures applied by other States if methods and materials recommended by WHO have been applied. The presence of vectors on board conveyances and the control methods used to eradicate them shall be included on the Ship Sanitation Control Certificate (Articles 22 and 24, and Annexes 3, 4 and 5).

Vector control in and around ports is also part of the IHR 2005. State Parties should ensure that port facilities are kept in a safe and sanitary condition and free from sources of infection and contamination, including vectors and reservoirs. The vector control measures should be extended to a minimum distance of 400 m from passenger terminals and operational areas (or more if vectors with a greater range are present, as documented in specific guidelines).

7.1.1 Health risks associated with vectors on ships

Control of disease vectors such as insects and rodents is necessary for the maintenance of health on board ships. Mosquitoes, rats, mice, cockroaches, flies, lice and rat fleas are all capable of transmitting disease.

Rodents are well established at port areas and are considered vectors for many diseases. Plague, murine typhus, salmonellosis, trichinosis, leptospirosis and rat bite fever are known to be spread by rodents.

Malaria is transmitted to humans by mosquito vectors. If not properly controlled, such vectors could breed and be carried by ships. Ships affected by malaria infection during a voyage represent a serious risk to health and life of crew and passengers. On board, the chances for early diagnosis and proper treatment are limited. Persons and vectors on board can, in turn, spread disease to ports (e.g. Delmont et al., 1994).

7.1.2 Standards

Article 20 of the IHR 2005 directs health authorities to ensure that ports have the "capacity" to inspect ships and then to issue either Ship Sanitation Control Certificates to direct disinfection or decontamination of the ship, including the control of vectors, or Ship Sanitation Control Exemption Certificates if contamination is not found.

Annex 1 of the IHR 2005 describes what constitutes this "capacity" and notes that this includes the capacity to derat, disinfect, disinsect and decontaminate ships.

Annex 4 of the IHR 2005 describes the process of issuance of such "certificates" and states that the presence of vectors, not necessarily evidence of disease per se, is sufficient basis for the issuance of the Ship Sanitation Control Certificate to decontaminate the ship of those vectors.

Annex 5 of the IHR 2005 describes the controls for vector-borne disease and provides health authorities with the right to control vectors found.

7.2 Guidelines

This section provides user-targeted information and guidance, identifying responsibilities and providing examples of practices that can control risks. Two specific *guidelines* (situations to aim for and maintain) are presented, each of which is accompanied by a set of *indicators* (measures for whether the guidelines are met) and *guidance notes* (advice on applying the guidelines and indicators in practice, highlighting the most important aspects that need to be considered when setting priorities for action).

Ports receive and manage goods and people from all over the world. Therefore, ports are exposed to the risk of vectors from any part of their country or any other port in the world. In addition, the activities undertaken at ports, such as handling foodstuffs, attract many species of vermin. On board ship, the relative isolation of passengers and crew from medical facilities makes diagnosis and treatment of disease more difficult and potentially increases the risk of serious harm. The relatively crowded nature of ships facilitates the spread of disease and ensures a concentration of foodstuffs and hosts for vectors.

Outbreaks associated with the presence of vectors on board are usually linked both to inadequate control and sanitation on board and to insufficient attention to preventing contamination in the first place. The failure of initial prevention leads to contamination, which is then exacerbated by failed ongoing control.

A preventive approach using good design that minimizes the opportunity for vector penetration, hiding and proliferation is the foundation of any good vector control strategy. Multiple barriers should be actively maintained, including:

- screening out vectors using all reasonable means;
- controlling vectors on board;
- eliminating habitats suitable for vector survival and breeding, where practicable;
- reducing the opportunity for exposure of passengers and crew to vector-related infectious agents.

One or more of the following control measures may be employed:

- regular inspection of ship spaces, particularly where infestation is most likely to occur, such as food storage, food handling and refuse disposal spaces;
- elimination of pest hiding places and point of accumulation in which trash, food particles or dirt may accumulate;
- frequent cleaning of living quarters and spaces where food is stored, prepared or served or in which dishes and utensils are washed and stored;
- proper storage and disposal of food refuse and rubbish (see chapter 3);
- elimination of habitat for insect larvae, ideally through design, or, if unavoidable, though maintenance, such as preventing the formation of standing water in lifeboats;
- use of screens on all structural openings to the outer air during seasons when insects are prevalent;
- application of suitable insecticides.

As vectors may have access to ships when in port, control measures for the suppression of vermin infestation are necessary. These control measures must be carried out under the direction of a ship's officer charged with this responsibility and must be frequently inspected.

7.2.1 Guideline 7.1: Insect vector control

Guideline 7.1—Insect vectors are controlled.

Indicators for Guideline 7.1

1. Insect-proof screens are used to prevent insect penetration.
2. Insecticides are used to control vector densities in air spaces and on surfaces.

Guidance notes for Guideline 7.1

1. Screens

Sleeping quarters, mess rooms and dining-rooms, indoor recreational areas and all food spaces must be effectively screened when ships are in areas where flies and mosquitoes are prevalent. Screening of sufficient hole tightness, no more than 1.6 mm spacing, is recommended, with screens on all outside openings. Screen doors should open outwards and be self-closing, and the screening must be protected from damage by heavy wire netting or other means, which may include the use of metal kick plates.

Ship holding water must be screened from insects and inspected frequently to check for, and eliminate, mosquito breeding. Refuse stores must be screened and inspected frequently to check for, and eliminate, the breeding of flies or other vermin.

Screens need to be kept in good repair. Bed nets, in good repair and properly placed, need to be used in sleeping quarters not provided with screens.

2. Insecticides

When leaving an area in which vectors are prevalent, and at regular intervals, residual and space sprays must be used for the control of flying insects that have entered the ship. Space sprays are released as a fog or fine mist and kill on contact. Residual sprays leave a deposit on surfaces where flying insects rest and where other insects crawl, and will remain active for a considerable period of time. Crawling insects and other vermin are best controlled by specific insecticides, properly applied to crawling, resting and hiding places.

As spray insecticides may contain substances toxic to humans, all surfaces that come in contact with food, all dishes and utensils and all food and drink need to be covered or removed during spraying operations.

Insecticides, rodenticides, any other poisonous substances and all equipment for their use must not be stored in or immediately adjacent to spaces used for storage, handling, preparation or serving of food or drink. Further, such poisonous substances should not be stored near dishes and utensils or tableware, linen and other equipment used for handling or serving food and drink. To prevent the accidental use of these poisons in foodstuffs, such hazards must be kept in coloured containers clearly marked as "POISON".

7.2.2 Guideline 7.2: Rodent vector control

Guideline 7.2—Rodent vectors are controlled.

Indicators for Guideline 7.2

1. Rodent proofing is installed and maintained.
2. Traps are used to control vector densities.
3. Poisoned baits are used to control vector densities.
4. Regular pest inspections are undertaken.
5. Hygienic practices are used to minimize rodent attractors.

Guidance notes for Guideline 7.2

1. Rodent proofing

Rats gain access to ships by various means, including direct access by hawsers (cables for mooring or towing the ship) and gangways. Others may be concealed in cargo, ships' stores and other materials taken onto the ship. However, the prevention of rat harbourage through appropriate construction and rat proofing will ensure almost complete control of rodents on board.

Some ships may be difficult to rat proof without major alterations. However, there are many rat-proofing measures that can be readily undertaken. These will materially reduce rat harbourage and will keep rat populations to a minimum after the ship has been deratted, provided that appropriate operational control measures on board ship are regularly followed.

Concealed spaces, structural pockets, openings that are too large (greater than 1.25 cm), leading to voids, food spaces and gaps around penetrating fixtures (e.g. pipes or ducts passing through bulkheads or decks), regardless of location, need to be obstructed with rat-proofing materials. The insulation layer around pipes, where over a certain thickness, 1.25 cm, needs to be protected against rat gnawing.

Rat-proofing materials should be robust and damage resistant. Such materials include sheet metal or alloy of suitable hardness and strength, wire mesh and hardware cloth.

Metal wire or sheet metal gauges must be of adequate strength and corrosion resistant. For example, aluminium should have a thickness by the Brown & Sharp gauge greater than the thickness specified by the United States standard for sheet iron, because aluminium is not as strong. For example, 16-gauge aluminium (Brown & Sharpe) might replace 18-gauge sheet iron (United States Standard). For grades of wire and hardware cloth, Washburn & Moen gauges are also used.

Certain non-rat-proof materials are satisfactory in rat-proof areas provided that the boundaries and various gnawing edges are flashed. Wood and asbestos composition materials are acceptable under conditions such as the following:

- Wood must be dry or seasoned and free of warps, splits and knots.
- Inorganic composition sheets and panels must be relatively strong and hard, with surfaces that are smooth and resistant to the gnawing of rats. A list of acceptable non-rat-proof materials may be obtained from national health administrations. If a new material is intended for use, the national health administration must be consulted in order to initiate approval procedures.
- Certain composition sheets and panels that do not meet the requirements in the bullet point above may be made acceptable by laminating with metal or facing on one side using suitable materials. All materials in this category are likely to be subject to health administration approval for inclusion in an acceptable non-rat-proof materials list.

Cements, putties, plastic sealing compounds, lead and other soft materials or materials subject to breaking loose are not advised in place of rat-proofing materials to close small openings. Firm, hard-setting materials used to close openings around cables within ferrules might need to be approved by the ship inspection officer. Fibreboards and plaster boards are generally not acceptable non-rat-proof materials. For approval, the relevant health administration should be consulted.

Non-rat-proof sheathing need not be rat proofed when placed flush against, or within 2 cm of, steel plate or when placed flush against rat-proofing material over insulation. Overlapping joints are not necessary for sheathing.

Effective rat-proofing collars at suitable distances from the ship and able to withstand wind action should be fitted to any hawsers that connect the ship to the shore.

2. Trapping

The master of the ship can delegate one person to be responsible for the vector control programme. Traps must be set after leaving any port where rats might have come on board either directly from the dock or with cargo or stores. If all traps are still empty after a period of two days, they can be taken up. If rats are caught, the traps in that area must be reset until no more rats are caught. A record of where the traps were set, the dates and results must be entered in the ship's log and a copy made available for the port health inspector.

3. Baiting

Most rodenticides may be very toxic and poisonous to humans. Caution must be used in their application, with instructions for their use carefully followed. The containers must be marked "POISON" and stored away from food preparation and storage areas; they must be coloured to prevent accidental use in food preparation. It should be checked that the baits have been correctly placed and whether they have been consumed.

4. Inspections

Rats leave droppings, gnawing damage and grease marks, which provide a ready indicator of infestation. Regular inspection of the ship to look for such evidence will show whether rats have gained access to the ship. Inspection should focus particularly on spaces where food is stored and prepared and where refuse is collected and disposed of, as well as the cargo hold while in port.

All rat proofing needs to be kept in good repair, inspected and maintained regularly. Pest infestations must be dealt with immediately and without adversely affecting food safety or suitability. Treatment with chemical, physical or biological agents must be carried out without posing a threat to the safety or suitability of food.

5. Hygiene

Rats pose a major threat to the safety and suitability of food. Rodent infestations can occur where there are breeding sites and a supply of food. Good hygiene practices should be employed to avoid creating an environment conducive to rodents. Good sanitation, inspection of incoming materials and good monitoring should minimize the likelihood of infestation and thereby limit the need for rodenticides.

8 Controlling infectious diseases in the environment

8.1 Background

This chapter deals with the management of persistent infectious agents on board ship.

8.1.1 Health risks associated with persistent infectious agents on ships

There have been a number of outbreaks of acute infectious gastrointestinal illnesses (AGI), such as those caused by norovirus (e.g. United States Centers for Disease Control and Prevention, 2002), and acute respiratory illnesses (ARI), such as influenza (e.g. Brotherton et al., 2003), on ships caused by communicable infectious agents. For example, in 2002, the United States Centers for Disease Control and Prevention detected 21 outbreaks (in this case, defined as "probable Norovirus infections causing illness in >3% of the ship population") on board ships arriving at ports in the United States (United States Centers for Disease Control and Prevention, 2002). In general, diseases arising from communicable infectious agents result from infection of the gastrointestinal system (digestive tract, intestines, stomach) and cause acute symptoms such as nausea, vomiting and diarrhoea. Respiratory infections can also arise and can cause acute symptoms such as fever, myalgia, weakness, sore throat, cold and cough. Although these diseases are often self-limiting or even asymptomatic, deaths can arise, particularly in sensitive populations. In the confines of a ship environment, these diseases can spread rapidly to affect significant proportions of the total ship population. These same diseases are highly prevalent on land, making it difficult to avoid some infected persons coming aboard.

The subject of this chapter is the infectious agents that have the ability to persist in air, water, vomitus and sputum and on surfaces for long enough that indirect transfer from one person to another can readily occur and result in an outbreak.

Many infectious agents can be spread via environmental surfaces and even via the air, including some protozoa, bacteria and viruses. However, to cause a detectable and significant outbreak on board, the agents need to be highly infectious and able to rapidly complete their incubation and begin replicating in their new infected host. For this reason, the environmentally persistent agents that cause AGI and ARI outbreaks on board ships are generally viruses. Our knowledge of these viruses and their taxonomy is rapidly evolving. However, in general, the risk factors and control measures to be applied on board are the same, regardless of the taxonomic classification of the infectious agent.

An infected person might, for example, be shedding an infectious agent via his or her faeces or vomitus. After bottom-wiping, nappy-changing or cleaning, the infected person or his or her caregiver might carry some of this material on their hands, unless thoroughly washed, leaving it on surfaces or in food or water that they touch around the ship. When another person touches those surfaces or consumes the food or water, he or she might pick up the infectious agent, which can then be ingested when putting fingers in the mouth or through ingestion of contaminated food or water.

Infectious agents can also be spread via the air, such as via coughing and sneezing, leading to exhaling of pathogens from the respiratory tract.

Waterborne and foodborne transmission of agents may also occur. This is considered in chapters 2 and 3, respectively, with particular discussion of the risks associated with *Legionella* spp.

This chapter considers two types of pathogens. Those infectious agents that cause AGI typically spread via environmental surfaces, such as door handles. Those infectious agents that cause ARI are more typically spread via the air.

Acute infectious gastrointestinal illnesses

Persistent infectious agents causing AGI are typically viruses belonging to the Calicivirus, Astrovirus and Reovirus families. These viruses are commonly associated with diarrhoea, with the Calicivirus family including the genus most commonly associated with ship-borne outbreaks: *Norovirus* (which has also been known as Norwalk-like virus and small round structured virus).

Because of the similarity between symptoms and control measures, and to illustrate the risk factors and control measures to be applied on board, norovirus will be used as a typical cause of AGI and influenza viruses as a typical cause of ARI. In general, norovirus is the more infectious, more resistant to disinfection and more difficult to control of these two types of virus and will form the primary focus of this chapter. For the most part, the controls in place to prevent norovirus spread on board will help reduce the spread of other, less robust pathogens among the persistent infectious agents.

Norovirus is considered to be the leading cause of adult gastroenteritis outbreaks worldwide and is thought to be second only to rotavirus in terms of all causes of gastroenteritis. Recent improvements in diagnostics and surveillance are likely to reveal more outbreaks on board ships. The probable role of international travellers as vectors was revealed by the similarity of strains between outbreaks across the world (White et al., 2002).

Norovirus can be transmitted by the aerosols liberated by projectile vomiting and therefore by airborne transmission (Marks et al., 2000) as well as by ingestion (both directly or indirectly via a surface) of infected vomit and faeces. Environmental surfaces can readily become contaminated and remain contaminated for some time (Cheesbrough et al., 2000).

An outbreak can spread rapidly throughout a ship, because norovirus has an incubation period of just 12–48 hours, and the proportion of those exposed that fall ill can be high (often above 50%) in all age groups (United States Centers for Disease Control and Prevention, 2002). Symptoms often start with sudden onset of projectile vomiting and/or diarrhoea. There may be fever, myalgia, abdominal cramps and malaise. Recovery occurs in 12–60 hours in most cases, and severe illness or mortality is rare, particularly if oral rehydration treatment is applied.

Because the infectious agents are persistent, outbreaks may continue and attack passengers and crew on successive voyages. Cohorts of new crew and passengers are introduced to the ship on a regular basis, so it is important to sanitize the ship after an outbreak.

Shedding rates for norovirus have been found to peak at above 10^6 virions per gram of faeces, dropping to around 1000 virions per gram of faeces three weeks from the cessation of symptoms in around 50% of cases and remaining detectable for up to seven weeks following the peak of infection (Tu et al., 2008). Therefore, even if ships are disinfected, bridging between groups may occur via a reservoir within infected persons. Another important implication of this prolonged shedding period, noting that it is often asymptomatic, is that some passengers and crew are likely to bring these persistent infectious agents on board with them regardless of what the crew does. It should be assumed that there are unrecognized infected individuals on board even in the absence of a detectable outbreak, and infection control precautions should be implemented continuously, not just after the outbreak has taken hold.

Acute respiratory illnesses

Persistent infectious agents causing ARI are typically viruses belonging to the Rhinovirus, Adenovirus, influenza virus and Coronavirus families. These viruses are commonly associated with symptoms such as cold and cough, and some cause broader symptoms resulting in greater morbidity, such as fever. Influenza viruses typically cause the most severe symptoms among the more commonly identified causes of outbreaks. Influenza viruses are an ongoing and common problem for ships due to the difficulty in containing their spread, even among partially vaccinated populations (Brotherton et al., 2003).

Severe acute respiratory syndrome (SARS) (WHO, 2004) has been noted as a disease that might be spread by travellers. This disease, caused by a coronavirus, has symptoms that are typically different from those of the gastrointestinal viruses described above and is associated with respiratory tract infection and flu-like symptoms. However, although initially presenting rather like influenza, complications can include severe pneumonia and respiratory system failure, which can be fatal. The risks from the person-to-person spread of SARS appear to be reduced by the same types of control measures applied for norovirus, influenza virus and similar agents.

In accordance with Article 37 of the IHR 2005, ships entering port may be required to report to health authorities on the health conditions on board during the voyage and the health status of passengers and crew. For this purpose, a Maritime Declaration of Health must be completed by the ship's master and countersigned by the ship's surgeon, if one is carried, and delivered to health officials after arrival.

8.2 Guidelines

This section provides user-targeted information and guidance, identifying responsibilities and providing examples of practices that should control risks. Three specific *guidelines* (situations to aim for and maintain) are presented, each of which is accompanied by a set of *indicators* (measures for whether the guidelines are met) and *guidance notes* (advice on applying the guidelines and indicators in practice, highlighting the most important aspects that need to be considered when setting priorities for action).

Risk factors for infection from communicable infectious agents are generally those that involve being in close proximity to an infected person, including (based on de Wit, Koopmans & van Duynhoven, 2003):

- having another infected person in the same family or group;
- coming into contact with an infected person;
- poor food and water handling hygiene;
- contact with both faeces and vomitus, which appear to be equally important;
- being in close proximity to a person who is infected and coughing or sneezing.

The significance of contact with other infected persons increases where the infected person is a young child.

Ships present a particularly high risk for extensive outbreaks, for several reasons. Many outbreaks on land have been associated with situations in which many people are in close proximity to other infected persons for a period of time, such as at parties, restaurants, schools and dormitories. These high-risk situations can all be present on a ship. Cabins often include people living in close proximity, often with children, who might otherwise be more separated.

The previous chapters in this guide emphasize prevention at source above all other control strategies. However, persistent infectious agents are typically so prevalent in the population, often without symptoms being evident, that it is not realistic to try to exclude infected individuals from coming on board. The focus of the control strategy for persistent infectious agents should be on taking all reasonable precautions to prevent transmission at all times; the working assumption should be that persons are infected. It is worth noting, however, that symptomatic individuals are typically far more infectious than those who are asymptomatic, and there is value in taking extra precautions relating to such individuals, seeking to minimize the possibility of patients contaminating others on board. Extended outbreaks may occur when there is inadequate control of possible infection pathways on board.

Reliance should not be placed on any single control strategy, and multiple barriers should be actively maintained.

8.2.1 Guideline 8.1: Transmission routes

Guideline 8.1—Transmission routes on board ship are minimized.

Indicators for Guideline 8.1

1. Good personal hygiene practices are promoted on board and required by crew and staff.
2. Stringent food and water hygiene is maintained on board.
3. Stringent hygiene practices with regard to cleaning and waste management on board are maintained.

Guidance notes for Guideline 8.1

1. Personal hygiene

Promoting and adopting good personal hygiene on board can significantly reduce the spread of persistent infectious agents. Examples of activities that should be promoted include:

- providing sufficient and ready access to hand-washing and sanitizing facilities at eateries, toilets, child-care facilities, health-care facilities and entry points, and keeping these facilities highly visible, including through the use of signage;
- providing non-contact facilities for hand washing, drying and sanitizing (e.g. taps and soap- and sanitizer-delivery systems that do not require hand contact to operate);
- avoiding putting fingers in or near the mouth unless first washed;
- avoiding placing objects that may have been touched into the mouth;
- providing guidance on proper hand washing and sanitizing;
- covering the nose and mouth with tissues when coughing or sneezing, which are then discarded.

2. Food and water hygiene

Promoting and adopting good food and water hygiene on board can significantly reduce the spread of persistent infectious agents. Examples of activities that should be promoted include:

- maintaining stringent food and water handling hygiene, as discussed in chapters 2 and 3 of this guide;
- designing self-service facilities to minimize infectious agent transmission, supervising these facilities closely and preventing children from using them; consider eliminating self-serve eating facilities during large outbreaks;

- limiting the need for indirect contact with others, such as the sharing of drink containers and eating utensils;
- providing separate serving utensils if dishes are to be shared, to avoid people serving themselves by hand or using utensils that have been placed in their mouths;
- providing cutlery and appropriate seating facilities to minimize the need to handle food while eating, and serving food of a type and packaged to minimize the need for handling;
- if food handling is inevitable as part of food consumption, providing hand sanitizers along with the food.

3. Good general hygiene practices

Adopting good hygiene practices should help to reduce the spread of persistent infectious agents on board. Examples of activities that should be promoted include:

- cleaning and sanitizing items both between and during voyages; this should include any environmental surface that might be touched by one infected person and lead to indirect transmission to another (toilet and tap operating handles; eating and drinking utensils; door handles; remote-control devices; switches on lights, radios and air-conditioning units; chair, table and bedding surfaces; and carpets);
- providing good ventilation;
- constructing surfaces from non-absorbent materials that are easily cleaned and sanitized;
- providing separate areas for children and adults to reduce the risk of cross-transmission;
- requiring the use of underwear or towels in saunas and other communal areas where clothing can otherwise be removed;
- rapidly cleaning up and sanitizing any faecal or vomitus spills on ship.

8.2.2 Guideline 8.2: Air quality

Guideline 8.2—Good air quality is maintained to reduce the risk of airborne disease transmission.

Indicator for Guideline 8.2

1. Good air quality is maintained to prevent airborne disease transmission.

Guidance notes for Guideline 8.2

To help protect air quality on board, it is important to keep air circulating and, as far as practicable, free from hazardous agents. Intake air openings should be maintained in clean and operational condition. Air filters should be kept in sanitary condition. Non-disposable (permanent) filters should be cleaned as recommended by the manufacturer, typically monthly. Disposable filters should be changed in accordance with the manufacturer's specification, typically every three months.

Air-conditioning rooms must be maintained in clean condition. Objects, chemicals, products and utensils should not be stocked or stored in these rooms, to avoid dispersion of biological or chemical hazards. Air-conditioning rooms should not present any leakage on condensing and cooling systems. Cleaning and disinfection procedures in the air-conditioning system should be made only with specific chemicals indicated for the specific system (non-toxic, biodegradable, etc.). Ship operators should monitor and record the cleaning and maintenance procedures for air-conditioning systems.

8.2.3 Guideline 8.3: Cases and outbreaks

Guideline 8.3—Cases and outbreaks are responded to effectively.

Indicators for Guideline 8.3

1. Procedures, equipment and facilities are in place to manage symptomatic individuals to minimize further disease spread.
2. Procedures, equipment and facilities are in place to respond to outbreaks with enhanced control measures.

Guidance notes for Guideline 8.3

1. Manage symptomatic individuals

The scope of this guide is as a "sanitation" guide. Refer to the WHO *International medical guide for ships* (WHO, 2007) and seek medical advice from the next port for case-by-case management for individuals.

Adopting targeted and additional controls around symptomatic individuals is justified given that they are likely to be highly infectious. Examples of activities that should be included in procedures include:

- putting in place systems to provide the earliest possible detection of disease symptoms;
- advising, or even requiring, symptomatic individuals to minimize contact with others;

- requesting that symptomatic individuals do not board the ship;
- wearing suitable masks and gloves while in close contact with symptomatic individuals;
- providing patients with advice on minimizing the risk of spreading their infection to others where they cannot be isolated, such as limiting any direct contact with others, even during greetings (e.g. shaking hands and kissing), remaining in cabins as much as possible to minimize contact with others and not taking part in food handling duties or other duties that may readily lead to transmission of infection;
- vaccinating crew that may come into contact with infected individuals, where practicable;
- using antiviral therapies, where available, to help suppress infection and shedding rates.

2. Respond to outbreaks

Enhanced responses to outbreaks should reduce their severity and duration and help to prevent outbreaks affecting subsequent travellers. Examples of activities that should be included in procedures include:

- seeking to identify the source of the outbreak. If the characteristic of an outbreak suggests a point source, the relevant control measures need to be rechecked and rigorously enforced, and epidemiological investigations should be undertaken to identify or exclude a food or water source. As foodborne and waterborne outbreaks have occurred on ships, kitchen hygiene practices and water safety management need to be reviewed and monitored;
- advising symptomatic passengers or crew to stay in cabins. Excretion and exhalation of viruses can begin shortly before the onset of symptoms and can continue for up to several weeks, although the maximum shedding typically occurs 24–72 hours after symptoms begin. The appropriate duration of confinement should be based on specific medical advice in accordance with the probable cause of disease;
- requiring cleaning staff and crew to undertake hand washing after contact with affected passengers or crew and objects, before handling food or drink and on leaving an affected area or cabin;
- requiring the wearing of suitable masks by crew and caregivers to protect those who come into contact with infected individuals;
- prompt cleaning and disinfection in areas contaminated by vomitus and faeces. Cleaning staff must wear gloves and aprons. Although there is evidence that airborne transmission is possible, the wearing of masks is generally not essential unless spattering or aerosolization is anticipated;

- separating embarking and disembarking passengers, if possible. If an outbreak has occurred on board, embarkation of new passengers should be delayed until the ship has been thoroughly cleaned and disinfected. The appropriate duration of separation should be based on specific medical advice in accordance with the specific nature of the disease.

Prolonged outbreaks on ships suggest that some infectious agents, such as norovirus, can be harboured in the ship environment. During an outbreak, there is a need for a comprehensive and responsive cleaning and disinfection programme during and at the end of an outbreak.

Particular attention must be given to cleaning objects that are frequently handled, such as taps, door handles, toilets or bath rails. For infectious agents causing AGI, the timing of the terminal cleaning process should be at least 72 hours after resolution of the last case. This takes into account the period of maximal infectivity (48 hours) plus the typical incubation period (24 hours) for the newly infected individuals. Affected areas should be cleaned and disinfected.

Contaminated linens and bed curtains must be placed carefully into laundry bags appropriate to guidelines for infected linens (e.g. soluble alginate bags with a colour-coded outer bag) without generating further aerosols. Contaminated pillows should be laundered as infected linen unless they are covered with an impermeable cover, in which case they must be disinfected.

Carpets and soft furnishings are particularly difficult to disinfect. Hypochlorite is not generally recommended, as prolonged contact is required, and many items requiring disinfection are not bleach resistant. Steam cleaning may be used for carpets and soft furnishings, provided that they are heat tolerant (some carpets are "bonded" to the underlying floor with heat-sensitive materials). However, this needs to be undertaken thoroughly, as a temperature of at least 60 °C is needed to achieve disinfection, and, in practice, tests have shown that such high temperatures are often not reached in carpets during steam cleaning. Vacuum cleaning carpets and buffing floors have the potential to recirculate viruses and are not recommended.

Contaminated hard surfaces should be washed with detergent and hot water, using a disposable cloth, then disinfected with a suitable disinfecting solution. Disposable cloths must be disposed of safely by handling so as not to contaminate other persons. Non-disposable mop heads and cleaning cloths must be laundered as contaminated linen using hot water.

Annex Examples of hazards, control measures, monitoring procedures and corrective actions for the ship water supply system

Source water

Hazard/ hazardous event	Control measure	Monitoring procedures	Corrective action
Contaminated source water	Routine checks on source water quality	Monitor turbidity and microbial indicators	Filter and disinfect, or use alternative source
Defective filters	Routine inspections and maintenance Regular backwashing and cleaning of filters	Monitor filter performance using turbidity	Repair or replace defective filters
Contaminated hoses	Regular cleaning and disinfection Regular repair and maintenance Proper storage and labelling	Routine inspections	Repair or replace Clean and disinfect
Contaminated hydrants	Regular cleaning and disinfection Regular repair and maintenance	Routine inspections	Repair or replace Clean and disinfect
Cross-connections with non-potable water at bunkering	Correct design and plumbing Correct labelling No connection with non-potable water	Routine inspections	Install new plumbing Isolate part of system Rechlorinate, flush
Defective backflow preventers at bunkering	No defects that allow ingress of contaminated water	Routine inspections, repair and maintenance	Repair or replace

Storage

Hazard/ hazardous event	Control measure	Monitoring procedures	Corrective action
Sediment at bottom of storage tanks	Routine cleaning (e.g. every 6 months)	Routine inspections, documentation	Procedure for cleaning storage tanks
Damage to wire mesh in overflow or vent pipe	Routine inspection, repair and maintenance	Routine sanitary inspections	Replace or repair
Cross-connections between potable water storage tank and non-potable water storage tank or pipe	Cross-connection control programme	Routine inspections, repair and maintenance	Repair or replace
Defects in potable water storage tanks	Routine sanitary inspection	Routine inspections, repair and maintenance	Repair or replace

Distribution system

Hazard/ hazardous event	Control measure	Monitoring procedures	Corrective action
Cross-connections with non-potable water	Prevent cross-connections Procedures for inspection, repair and maintenance Correct identification of pipes and tanks	Routine inspections	Break cross-connection
Defective pipes, leaks	Procedures for inspection, repair and maintenance	Routine inspections	Repair pipes
Defective backflow preventers at outlets throughout distribution system	No defects that would allow ingress of contaminated water	Routine inspections Testing of preventers	Repair or replace

Distribution system *continued*

Hazard/ hazardous event	Control measure	Monitoring procedures	Corrective action
Contamination during repair and maintenance of tanks and pipes	No defects that would allow ingress into potable water tanks or pipes Procedures for hygienic repair and maintenance Procedures for cleaning and disinfection	Inspection of job Water sampling (microbiological analysis)	Train staff Written procedures Disinfect fracture area and fitting
Leaking pipes or tanks	Prevention of leakage System maintenance and renewal	Routine inspections Pressure and flow monitoring	Repair
Toxic substances in pipe materials	No toxic substances Specifications for pipe materials	Check specifications for pipes and materials Check specification certificates	Replace pipes if specification is not correct
Insufficient residual disinfection	Adequate to prevent regrowth (e.g. maintaining free chlorine residual above 0.2 mg/l)	Online monitoring of residual, pH and temperature Routine sampling	Investigate cause and rectify

Glossary

Acceptable non-rat-proof material	A material whose surface is resistant to gnawing by rats when exposed edges are flashed, but which can be subject to penetration by rats if the gnawing edges are not so protected.
Accessible	Capable of being exposed for cleaning and inspection with the use of simple tools such as a screwdriver, pliers or an open-end wrench.
Air gap	The unobstructed vertical distance through the free atmosphere between the lowest opening from any pipe or faucet supplying water to a tank, plumbing fixture or other device and the flood-level rim of the receptacle or receiving fixture. The air gap must be at least twice the diameter of the supply pipe or faucet or at least 2.5 cm.
Backflow	The flow of water or other liquids, mixtures or substances into the distribution pipes of a potable supply of water from any source or sources other than the potable water supply. Back-siphonage is one form of backflow.
Backflow preventer	An approved backflow-prevention plumbing device that must be used on potable water distribution lines where there is a direct connection or a potential connection between the potable water distribution system and other liquids, mixtures or substances from any source other than the potable water supply. Some devices are designed for use under continuous water pressure, whereas others are non-pressure types.
Corrosion resistant	Able to resist corrosive deterioration so that the surface maintains its original surface characteristics even under prolonged influence of the intended use environment.
Coved	A concave surface, moulding or other design that eliminates the usual angles of 90 degrees or less so as to prevent the accumulation of dirt and debris and facilitate cleaning.
Crew	Persons on board a conveyance who are not passengers.
Cross-connection	Any unprotected actual or potential connection or structural arrangement between a public or a consumer's potable water system and any other source or system through which it is possible to introduce into any part of the potable system any used water, industrial fluid, gas or substance other than the intended potable water with which the system is supplied. Bypass arrangements, jumper connections, removable sections, swivel or change-over devices and other temporary or permanent devices that can allow backflow are considered to be cross-connections.
Deck sink	A sink recessed into the deck, usually located at tilting kettles and pans.

Easily cleanable	Fabricated with a material, finish and design that allow for easy and thorough cleaning with normal cleaning methods and materials.
Flashing	The capping or covering of corners, boundaries and other exposed edges of acceptable non-rat-proof material in rat-proof areas. The flashing strip must be of rat-proof material, wide enough to cover the gnawing edges adequately and firmly fastened.
Floor sink	*See* Deck sink.
Food contact surfaces	Surfaces of equipment and utensils with which food normally comes in contact and surfaces from which food may drain, drip or splash back onto surfaces normally in contact with food; this includes the areas of ice machines over the ice chute to the ice bins. (*See also* Non-food contact surfaces.)
Food handling areas	Any area where food is stored, processed, prepared or served.
Food preparation areas	Any area where food is processed, cooked or prepared for service.
Food service areas	Any area where food is presented to passengers or crew members (excluding individual cabin service).
Food storage areas	Any area where food or food products are stored.
Greywater	Drainage water from galleys, dishwashers, showers, laundries, baths and washbasins. It does not include sewage, medical wastewater or bilge water from the machinery spaces.
Health-based target	A benchmark to guide progress towards a predetermined health or water safety goal. There are four types of health-based targets: health outcome targets, water quality targets, performance targets and specified technology targets.
Maximum opening	The largest opening through which a rat cannot pass, applicable to both rat-proof and rat-tight areas. Regardless of the shape of the opening, it would normally be 1.25 cm or less in the minimum dimension.
Non-absorbent materials	Those materials whose surface is resistant to the absorption of moisture.
Non-food contact surfaces	All exposed surfaces, other than food contact or splash contact surfaces, of equipment located in food storage, preparation and service areas.
Portable	A description of equipment that is readily removable or mounted on casters, gliders or rollers; provided with a mechanical means so that it can be tilted safely for cleaning; or readily movable by one person.

Potable water	Fresh water that is intended for human consumption, such as drinking, washing, teeth brushing, bathing or showering; for use in freshwater recreational water environments; for use in the ship's hospital; for handling, preparing or cooking food; and for cleaning food storage and preparation areas, utensils and equipment. Potable water, as defined by the WHO Guidelines for drinking-water quality, does not represent any significant risk to health over a lifetime of consumption, including different sensitivities that may occur between life stages.
Potable water tanks	All tanks in which potable water is stored from bunkering and production for distribution and use as potable water.
Rat-proof area	An area that is completely isolated from other areas by means of rat-proof material or by design.
Rat-proof material	A material whose surface and edges are resistant to the gnawing of rats.
Readily removable	Capable of being detached from the main unit without the use of tools.
Removable	Capable of being detached from the main unit with the use of simple tools such as a screwdriver, pliers or an open-end wrench.
Scupper	A conduit or collection basin that channels water runoff to a drain.
Sealant	Material used to fill seams to prevent the entry or leakage of liquid or moisture.
Seam	An open juncture between two similar or dissimilar materials. Continuously welded junctures, ground and polished smooth, are not considered seams.
Sewage	Any liquid waste that contains human, animal or vegetable matter in suspension or solution, including liquids that contain chemicals in solution.
Ship	A seagoing or inland navigation vessel on an international or national voyage.
Utility sink	Any sink located in a food service area not used for hand washing and/or dishwashing.

References

Bartram J et al., eds (2007). *Legionella and the prevention of legionellosis.* Geneva, World Health Organization (http://www.who.int/water_sanitation_health/emerging/legionella.pdf, accessed 30 January 2011).

Bartram J et al. (2009). *Water safety plan manual: step-by-step risk management for drinking-water suppliers.* Geneva, World Health Organization (http://whqlibdoc.who.int/publications/2009/9789241562638_eng.pdf, accessed 30 January 2011).

Brotherton JML et al. (2003). A large outbreak of influenza A and B on a cruise ship causing widespread morbidity. *Epidemiology and Infection*, 130(2):263–271.

Cheesbrough JS et al. (2000). Widespread environmental contamination with Norwalk-like viruses (NLV) detected in a prolonged hotel outbreak of gastroenteritis. *Epidemiology and Infection*, 125(1):93–98.

Cruise Lines International Association (2010). *The contribution of the North American cruise industry to the U.S. economy in 2009.* Prepared by Business Research and Economic Advisors for the Cruise Lines International Association.

Delmont J et al. (1994). Harbour-acquired *Plasmodium falciparum* malaria. *The Lancet*, 344(8918):330–331.

de Wit MAS, Koopmans MPG, van Duynhoven YTHP (2003). Risk factors for norovirus, Sapporo-like virus, and group A rotavirus gastroenteritis. *Emerging Infectious Diseases* [serial online], December 2003 (http://www.cdc.gov/ncidod/EID/vol9no12/02-0076.htm, accessed 30 January 2011).

Falkinham JO III (2003). Mycobacterial aerosols and respiratory disease. *Emerging Infectious Diseases* [serial online], July 2003 (http://www.cdc.gov/ncidod/eid/vol9no7/02-0415.htm, accessed 30 January 2011).

FAO/WHO (1995). *Codex Alimentarius: Vol. 1B—General requirements (food hygiene).* Rome, Food and Agriculture Organization of the United Nations and World Health Organization, Joint FAO/WHO Food Standards Programme, Codex Alimentarius Commission.

FAO/WHO (1997a). *Codex Alimentarius: Supplement to volume 1B—General requirements (food hygiene)*, 2nd ed. Rome, Food and Agriculture Organization of the United Nations and World Health Organization, Joint FAO/WHO Food Standards Programme, Codex Alimentarius Commission.

FAO/WHO (1997b). *Codex Alimentarius: Food hygiene—Basic texts—General principles of food hygiene, HACCP guidelines, and guidelines for the establishment of microbiological criteria for foods.* Rome, Food and Agriculture Organization of the United Nations and World Health Organization, Joint FAO/WHO Food Standards Programme, Codex Alimentarius Commission.

FAO/WHO (1999). *Codex Alimentarius: Vol. 1A—General requirements*, 2nd ed., revised. Rome, Food and Agriculture Organization of the United Nations and World Health Organization, Joint FAO/WHO Food Standards Programme, Codex Alimentarius Commission.

FAO/WHO (2001). *General standard for bottled/packaged drinking waters (other than natural mineral waters)*. Rome, Food and Agriculture Organization of the United Nations and World Health Organization, Joint FAO/WHO Food Standards Programme, Codex Alimentarius Commission (Codex Standard 227-2001; http://www.codexalimentarius.net/download/standards/369/CXS_227e.pdf, accessed 30 January 2011).

FAO/WHO (2003). *Recommended international code of practice—General principles of food hygiene.* Rome, Food and Agriculture Organization of the United Nations and World Health Organization, Joint FAO/WHO Food Standards Programme, Codex Alimentarius Commission (CAC/RCP1-1969, Rev. 4-2003; http://www.codexalimentarius.net/download/standards/23/cxp_001e.pdf, accessed 30 January 2011).

Gustafson TL et al. (1983). *Pseudomonas* folliculitis: an outbreak and review. *Reviews of Infectious Diseases*, 5:1–8.

IHS Fairplay (2010). *World fleet statistics 2009*. IHS Global Ltd.

IMO (1998). *Guidelines for the control and management of ships' ballast water to minimize the transfer of harmful aquatic organisms and pathogens*. London, International Maritime Organization.

IMO (2009). *International shipping and world trade facts and figures, October 2009.* International Maritime Organization, Maritime Knowledge Centre (http://www.imo.org/KnowledgeCentre/ShippingFactsAndNews/TheRoleandImportanceofInternationalShipping/Documents/International%20Shipping%20and%20World%20Trade%20-%20facts%20and%20figures%20oct%202009%20rev1__tmp65768b41.pdf, accessed 30 January 2011).

IMO (2010). Life-Saving Appliance Code. In: *Life-saving appliances*, 2010 ed. London, International Maritime Organization.

Lemmon JM, McAnulty JM, Bawden-Smith J (1996). Outbreak of cryptosporidiosis linked to an indoor swimming pool. *Medical Journal of Australia*, 165:613.

Lew JF et al. (1991). An outbreak of shigellosis aboard a cruise ship caused by a multiple-antibiotic-resistant strain of *Shigella flexneri. American Journal of Epidemiology*, 134(4):413–420.

Marks PJ et al. (2000). Evidence for airborne transmission of Norwalk-like virus (NLV) in a hotel restaurant. *Epidemiology and Infection*, 124:481–487.

National Advisory Committee on Microbiological Criteria for Foods (1997). *Hazard analysis and critical control point principles and application guidelines.* Washington, DC, United States Department of Health and Human Services (http://www.fda.gov/Food/FoodSafety/HazardAnalysisCriticalControlPointsHACCP/ucm114868.htm, accessed 30 January 2011).

Ratnam S et al. (1986). Whirlpool associated folliculitis caused by *Pseudomonas aeruginosa*: report of an outbreak and review. *Journal of Clinical Microbiology*, 23:655–659.

Rooney RM et al. (2004). A review of outbreaks of waterborne disease associated with ships: evidence for risk management. *Public Health Reports*, 119:435–442.

Temeshnikova ND et al. (1996). The presence of *Legionella* spp. in the water system of ships. In: Berdal B, ed. *Legionella infections and atypical pneumonias. Proceedings of the 11th meeting of the European Working Group on Legionella Infections, Oslo, Norway, June 1996.* Oslo, Norwegian Defence Microbiological Laboratory.

Tu ETV et al. (2008). Norovirus excretion in an aged-care setting. *Journal of Clinical Microbiology*, 46:2119–2121.

United Kingdom Food Standards Agency (2009). *Food handlers: fitness to work. Regulatory guidance and best practice advice for food business operators.* London, Food Standards Agency (http://www.food.gov.uk/multimedia/pdfs/publication/fitnesstoworkguide09v3.pdf, accessed 30 January 2011).

United Nations (2008). *Review of maritime transport.* Geneva, United Nations Conference on Trade and Development (Publication UNCTAD/RMT/2008).

United States Centers for Disease Control and Prevention (1996). Lake-associated outbreak of *Escherichia coli* O157:H7—Illinois, 1995. *Morbidity and Mortality Weekly Report,* 45(21):437–439.

United States Centers for Disease Control and Prevention (2000). *Pseudomonas* dermatitis/folliculitis associated with pools and hot tubs—Colorado and Maine, 1999–2000. *Morbidity and Mortality Weekly Report,* 49(48):1087–1091.

United States Centers for Disease Control and Prevention (2001a). Protracted outbreaks of cryptosporidiosis associated with swimming pool use—Ohio and Nebraska, 2000. *Morbidity and Mortality Weekly Report,* 50(20):406–410.

United States Centers for Disease Control and Prevention (2001b). Shigellosis outbreak associated with an unchlorinated fill-and-drain wading pool—Iowa, 2001. *Morbidity and Mortality Weekly Report,* 50(37):797–800.

United States Centers for Disease Control and Prevention (2002). Outbreaks of gastroenteritis associated with noroviruses on cruise ships—United States. *Morbidity and Mortality Weekly Report,* 51:1112.

White P et al. (2002). Norwalk-like virus 95/96-US strain is a major cause of gastroenteritis outbreaks in Australia. *Journal of Medical Virology,* 68(1):113–118.

WHO (1997). *Guidelines for drinking-water quality,* 2nd ed. *Vol. 3. Surveillance and control of community supplies.* Geneva, World Health Organization (http://www.who.int/water_sanitation_health/dwq/gdwqvol32ed.pdf, accessed 30 January 2011).

WHO (1999). *Guidelines for safe disposal of unwanted pharmaceuticals in and after emergencies: interagency guidelines.* Geneva,

World Health Organization (WHO/EDM/PAR/99.2; http://www.who.int/water_sanitation_health/medicalwaste/unwantpharm.pdf, accessed 30 January 2011).

WHO (2001). *Sanitation on ships. Compendium of outbreaks of foodborne and waterborne disease and Legionnaires' disease associated with ships 1970–2000*. Geneva, World Health Organization (WHO/SDE/WSH/01.4; http://www.who.int/water_sanitation_health/hygiene/ships/en/shipsancomp.pdf, accessed 30 January 2011).

WHO (2004). *WHO guidelines for the global surveillance of severe acute respiratory syndrome (SARS). Updated recommendations. October 2004*. Geneva, World Health Organization (WHO/CDS/CSR/ARO/2004.1; http://www.who.int/csr/resources/publications/WHO_CDS_CSR_ARO_2004_1.pdf, accessed 30 January 2011).

WHO (2005). *Revision of the International Health Regulations*. Geneva, World Health Organization, Fifty-eighth World Health Assembly (WHA58.3, Agenda item 13.1, 23 May 2005; http://whqlibdoc.who.int/publications/2008/9789241580410_eng.pdf, accessed 30 January 2011).

WHO (2006). *Guidelines for safe recreational water environments. Vol. 2. Swimming pools and similar environments*. Geneva, World Health Organization (http://www.who.int/water_sanitation_health/bathing/srwe2full.pdf, accessed 30 January 2011).

WHO (2007). *International medical guide for ships*, 3rd ed. Geneva, World Health Organization.

WHO (2009). *Guide to hygiene and sanitation in aviation*, 3rd ed. *Module 1: Water; Module 2: Cleaning and disinfection of facilities*. Geneva, World Health Organization (http://www.who.int/water_sanitation_health/hygiene/ships/guide_hygiene_sanitation_aviation_3_edition.pdf, accessed 30 January 2011).

WHO (2010). *International Health Regulations (2005). Recommended procedures for inspection of ships and issuance of Ship Sanitation Certificates*. Draft document. Geneva, World Health Organization (http://www.who.int/ihr/ports_airports/ssc_guide_draft_27_may_2010.pdf, accessed 30 January 2011).

WHO (2011). *Guidelines for drinking-water quality*, 4th ed. Geneva, World Health Organization (in press).